A Guide for Actors New to Television

Tristan de Vere Cole

A Guide for Actors New to Television

Illustrated by Diana de Vere Cole

A Nadder Book

ELEMENT BOOKS LTD

© Tristan de Vere Cole 1985
First Published in Great Britain 1985 by
Element Books Ltd
Longmead Shaftesbury Dorset

ISBN 0 906540 70 4

Set in Palatino by
Characters, Chard, Somerset
Printed by Billings, Hylton Road, Worcester

Cover illustration by Diana de Vere Cole
Cover and text design by Humphrey Stone

Contents

Introduction

In spite of the increase in electronics and technical wizardry, it is the human factor that is the most important element in the making of programmes for television.

Television Drama is above all a team effort. You, as Actors, are vital members of that team. Even though you join a production well after preparation for the project has started, you are the ones that the public see on the screen. It is through your interpretation of the script that the audience identifies with a programme's content.

The arrival of Cable and Satellite television seems to have reinforced the old adage that television is an Engineer's medium – in comparison to the theatre being an Actor's, and film a Director's medium. This is not strictly true. However, there will be times when you will feel very much at the mercy of the Technicians. They can distort your image and voice, they can light you to look like Dracula or, hopefully, a Saint. They can twiddle a knob to make you go green or purple; they can suggest that you strike an attitude that will give them a lovely picture, but which is totally alien to the character that you are portraying. Therefore, although the build up, planning and organisation that go into making a programme are rather like the base of an iceberg, and there is a great deal of which you will never be aware, it is important that you have some idea of how the production personnel and technical crews, in both film and electronic studio, operate and think, so that you, the Actor, can benefit from their contributions.

This Guide travels the road from "Attempting to get an interview", to the "Completion of the final studio scene"; incorporating hints, tips, dos and don'ts, with descriptions of the jobs of the television personnel that the

Actor will meet en route.

Despite the use of the male gender, it must be emphasised that women work at nearly every job mentioned; though I have yet to meet a woman armourer.

After a talk given at the Actors Centre, when it was at Covent Garden*, it was suggested that Drama Students and Actors who had not yet worked in Television would find a printed version of my notes helpful. I hope that this now proves to be the case.

Tristan de Vere Cole

---

*The Actors Centre is now situated at: 4 Chenies Street, London EC1E 7EP

1 Getting an Interview

There are a number of avenues leading to that all important step – 'Getting an Interview'.

Letters

The sending of your curriculum vitae and photographs to Producers, Directors and Casting Directors can be a depressing and expensive chore, but it can be worthwhile. Although you will very rarely get a 'General Interview' with a Producer or Director, and will only be seen if there is a specific part for which you may be suitable, there is the possibility that your information may arrive on a Director's desk at an opportune time, when a specific qualification listed in your C.V. is required – pilot, parachutist, skin-diver, show jumper, typist, rollerskater, etc.

Obviously mention any qualification that may help you get an interview. For example: if you have heard that a Director is casting for a thriller series with underwater archaeology as a background, a letter on the following lines is sensible:

> Dear Albert Snodgrass,
> I believe that you are casting for a series about under-water archaeology. I enclose a photograph and my curriculum vitae and hope that I can meet you.
> I am a fully qualified diver to a depth of fifty metres and helped raise "The Mary Rose".
> The beard is optional – there is a clean shaven photograph in *Spotlight*.
> > Yours sincerely,

As a general rule letters should be kept short and addressed either: Dear Mr .... or Dear Christian name and surname. If you attempt witty comments, in the hope that they may attract attention, make sure that they are winners – facetious remarks can hinder not help.

Do not enclose a stamped addressed envelope; the B.B.C. and other Television Companies can afford the return postage.

When you are going to be appearing in a theatre production or film, a letter to the Head of Casting of each of the Independent Companies, with words to the effect that: "I would be grateful if you would let your Casting Directors know that I am appearing as .... in......... at.......... on........," may reap dividends.

To send a similar letter to all the Directors working with the major Independent Companies and to the sixty or so Directors currently working at the B.B.C. – let alone those working in the Regional Centres at Birmingham, Bristol, Cardiff and Glasgow – is more of a long shot. There are no Casting Directors at the B.B.C. To obtain a list of Directors working at the B.B.C. London, ring 01 743 8000 and ask for the Management Assistant, Series and Serials, and on a separate extension, the Plays Department.

If you deliver a batch of letters to the Mail Room at the B.B.C. Television Centre, they will be distributed internally, and this will obviously save on postage.

Contacts published annually by *Spotlight*, gives a comprehensive list of the addresses and telephone numbers at all the B.B.C. Centres and Independent Television Companies. When ringing the Regional Centres you should ask for the Drama Department.

For your first television production, it is worth having a card printed for maximum circulation.

Never expect a reply to your letters.

Spotlight

This four volume publication appears annually, and advertises photographs of Artists. It is extensively used by production personnel and is a very sound investment. It is wise to have a look at a copy to see the sort of photographs used: modern, head only or head and shoulders. Even if you have good legs, it is unwise to publish a full length photograph, especially in the quarter pages section, where your face will be too small. An accurate representation of your features is better than an over-glamorized one that hides the size of your nose; but do not publish a snapshot taken in your backyard. Always detail your height, and the year of the photograph. It is also helpful to say who took it, and the colour of your eyes. If you have no Agent's address to put alongside your photograph you can be contacted c/o *The Spotlight*, provided that you keep them up to date with your whereabouts. The current *Spotlight* address is: 42-43 Cranbourn Street, London WC2H 7AP. Tel. 01 437 7631.

The Agent

The Agent's business is to be in the 'know' about productions in preparation, and to suggest his clients for any suitable work. Because he is aware of current fees, he is able to negotiate the best deal on your behalf; true it is also on his own behalf, because the higher the fee the higher his commission, but even if he takes 15% (the average is 10%) you will probably end up with more than if you had negotiated your own contract. Sometimes the Agent is approached by a Director for an Actor in his *stable* and is able to say: "Sorry that Actor is not available, but a brilliant chap has just joined us from drama school, and I think that you should see him."

Agents occasionally receive a *character breakdown* for a production. This detailed list of casting requirements is sent by the Director, particularly when working for the B.B.C., in order to elicit suggestions and to save repetitive descriptions on the telephone.

Although there are Actors who operate successfully without an Agent, they are rare, and when starting your career it is better to have an Agent who may be low in the league, than no Agent at all.

5

Some Agents come to see Drama School productions and may approach you to join them. Others may be rather grand and only deal with established names. *Contacts* has a list of over one hundred and fifty Actors' Agents. Your Drama School and friends in the business should be able to advise you about which ones to write to, and which should be avoided. If you are approached by more than one Agent, find out who they have got on their books – this may help you to assess which one to join.

If you are not at a Drama School, and have no Agent, you may find it difficult to get one to come and see your work – but keep pestering – even if it is to see you busking in Leicester Square, or performing cabaret in a club or pub.

Personal Video Tapes

If well presented, personal promotion tapes can be useful and a good investment, but the capital outlay may be beyond some Actors. Should you decide to make a demonstration tape, which can be sent to potential Agents, as well as Producers, Directors and Casting Directors, keep it short – say twelve to fifteen minutes – and in that time try to put across your many talents in a few short pieces, working your skills, such as singer, pianist and linguist into your dramatic selection, but only if they are of a high standard. Keep attempts at accents to those with which you are completely at home.

Start by showing yourself with no make-up, and give a run-down of your programme to camera. This is primarily to give the viewer an idea of what you look like and how you sound with your natural accent. To launch into your favourite theatre audition of Henry V's speech at Agincourt may be counter productive.

It is a worthwhile thought to share a tape with another Actor; thereby halving the main cost. Playing two hander scenes with a partner will help your performance. It is also possible to 'bounce off' another player, who need only be seen occasionally with his back to camera – the camera favouring you throughout.

Do not compile an amateur tape. It needs to be slickly directed, edited and presented with all the expertise and advice of the professional.

There are video companies who advertise in Theatrical and Television magazines and papers such as: *The Stage and Television Today*, but see an example of their work before committing yourself. Talk to those friends and fellow Actors whose advice you respect. Word of mouth is probably the best recommendation. Foremost in the field is *Video Casting Directory* whose current address is: Studios 8 and 9, Royal Victoria Patriotic Building, Trinity Road, London sw18 3sx. Tel. 01 870 3023 and 01 874 0087. They are specialists in this form of presentation, provide all facilities – studio, editing etc. – and will make copies of your promotion tape, so that you can send it to a variety of people. They also operate a form of mobile spotlight to help production companies when casting. Compilation video tapes, which have 3 minute sections of a number of Actors, are sent out with a photographic brochure. Directors can then spin the video cassette to whoever they want to see. This form of video promotion, although not as personal as the individually made tape, is obviously cheaper, and has the advantage of a wide distribution to a number of potential employers.

Casting Information

The Stage and Television Today often gives information about forthcoming television drama productions and *P.C.R.* (Professional Casting Report), is a weekly publication listing who is casting what, when and where.

P.C.R.'s current address is: 280 Lordship Lane, London se22. Tel. 01 693 2866. However, you would be wise to check cost, and seek advice from past or present users, before becoming a subscriber.

'Job Grapevine' is a free service for Equity members only. Details of how it operates can be obtained from the Equity Offices, 8 Harley Street, London w1a 2ab. Tel. 01 636 6367.

If you become a member of The Actors Centre, 4 Chenies Street wc1, or a group like The Actors Workshop, 6 Denmark Street, wc2, then you are likely to glean useful casting information.

To Be Or Not To Be An 'Extra'

"If I accept work as a non-speaking crowd artist, will this prejudice my future chances of a proper role?" Whilst at Drama School take every opportunity to be an 'Extra'. You will see and learn a great deal, even from one day's work. Thereafter try to avoid the role of non-speaking artist.

It is possible to be elevated from the crowd to speak a word or two, and so be noticed for future work; David Niven began in the crowd, and Audrey Hepburn in the chorus line, but the golden age of Hollywood is past, and such stories are rare now. You can easily get labelled and then find it hard to break out of the rut, and there is an existing core of supporting crowd artists, who are known to be reliable enough for the occasional small part.

If a specific crowd is required, i.e. 'Students', and the Agencies cannot provide enough of their own clients, the T.V. companies are allowed to use Drama Students. If productions, which are taking place away from London require crowd artists, then local students, (Drama or otherwise), and non Equity members may be employed; provided that all known local Equity members have already been approached.

Casting Directors (I.T.V.) Artists Bookers (B.B.C.)

The Independent Companies' system of appointing Casting Directors who are expected to find new faces and new talent, as well as to suggest ideas to Directors, is undoubtedly sensible. At the B.B.C. the Director has no such help; he is allocated an Artists Booker who, although sometimes helpful with casting suggestions when asked, is not expected to be a talent scout or to put up ideas. His job is to *book* the Actor, having received instructions from the Director's office.

8

To be or not to be an extra

There is a Casting Advisory department at the B.B.C. that interviews, and sometimes video tapes auditions, but it is, at present, underused by Directors.

At Independent Companies the Casting Director meets

the Director; they discuss ideas, and then the Casting Director checks Actors' availability for the production dates, before arranging interviews.

At the B.B.C., Producer and Director will work closely on casting; discussing ideas and commenting on each other's suggestions before the Production Assistant, who works in the Director's office, fixes a date, time, and place for an interview with the Director.

In a long running series, when there will be more than one Director, the *Regulars* will be cast by the Producer and the *Guest* parts for each episode by the Director.

What is the difference between a Producer and a Director, and what does an Executive Producer do?

The Producer is normally a member of staff and is primarily the Management's representative. Some have been Directors, others have been Production Managers, Department Organisers or Script Editors. He may be producing a programme that he has conceived or he may be allocated a project by his Head of Department. He will meet the Author at any early stage to discuss and suggest ideas.

Amongst many functions he is the money man, responsible for quality, economy and efficiency. Without the money there can be no programme, and he has to be sure that sufficient funds have been allowed to realise the agreed concept.

The Producer is also responsible for promotion, publicity and dealing with any legal problems, as well as booking the technical resources, facilities and staff. He acts as a catalyst, trying to bring together the best personnel available from the various staff servicing departments. He is looking, preferably in discussion with the Director, for a production and technical team that will work well with the Director and in harmony together. The fiery or moody artistic temperament is not confined to those in front of the camera, indeed, contrary to public belief, technical staff are sometimes not as disciplined or as tolerant as Actors.

10

Usually the Producer is the one who tries to find the right Director for the script, and naturally the Producer/Director relationship is of the utmost importance. The Director must agree to work within his allocated budget, and they must both agree on the overall style of the programme. The Producer will endeavour to help smooth the path of the Director in every aspect.

The B.B.C. Producer has help from a *Production Associate* who is very much involved in the basic planning and the provision of post production facilities, and is particularly concerned with money; making sure that the programme stays within its allocated budget. The B.B.C. Producer also has the assistance of a *Script Editor*, of whom more later.

There are increasing instances of a creative package – Script, Director and Lead Actors – being offered to T.V. Companies. Sometimes this package will include a Producer, now freelance, who may have worked previously with the company concerned, and will therefore know how it operates, and the personnel within it.

The Director is nearly always freelance. Many have had theatre experience, either as Actors or in Stage Management, before joining a Television Directors Training Course, or starting at a lower level in production teams; but some have been Documentary Film makers, Cameramen, Film Editors, Designers or Vision Mixers.

The prime function of the Director is the artistic interpretation of the script, allied to the craft of presenting it in television terms as efficiently as possible, with the technical and human resources at his disposal.

He is responsible for the selection of Actors, and planning of rehearsals, location and studio work. The Producer has tried to get him the best Designer, Costume Designer, Make-up Artist, Lighting, Sound and Camera Crew, as well as his immediate production team of Production Manager and Assistants, and these will now work to the Director. They are, so to speak, his orchestra, with you the

Actors as soloists. He is the conductor trying to stimulate everybody's talents and creativity. Sometimes the various departments can pull in different directions and he is like a coachman trying to control eight horses along the road he wants to go.

The Director will try to create an atmosphere in which an Actor can give of his best.

The Executive Producer (I.T.V.) Head of Department (B.B.C.) You may never see him. Normally he has control of a number of Series/Serials or Plays. He is the Producer's boss, and is responsible to the Controller of Programmes or Head of Channel.

2 The Interview

Your interview for an I.T.V. Company will probably be in a quiet, civilised office with just the Director and Casting Director present.

At the B.B.C. you may be seen by the Director and Producer, by the Director alone, or just as likely in a crowded, busy office.

Dress

Regard the coming interview as an investment for the future. Be yourself, and do not necessarily go dressed for the

Do not necessarily go dressed for the part

part, as the Director may feel that you are underestimating his powers of judgement. However, if your Agent tells you that you are going up for the part of an Officer Cadet or a Secretary at the Foreign Office it is sensible not to go looking scruffy. When being seen for Commercials, it is probably wise to make a subtle effort to look the part. Actresses tend to believe that the choice of clothes for an interview is more important for women than men, and they may be right.

Photographs

Your Agent will have sent the Director a photograph when he suggested you for the part, or you may have sent a selection with your C.V., but assume that they will have been mislaid. Always take photographs that can be left behind if necessary as an aide memoire. Very large ones will be more of a handicap than a help, postcard size will be adequate.

If you have only one photograph and it is the same as the one you have published in *Spotlight*, still bring it, as it saves the Director having to refer to one of the heavy volumes. The full length photograph that displays your figure may be useful if you are being interviewed for the part of a disco dancer or club hostess.

Always remember to put your name, address and Agent on the back of the photographs – you would be surprised how many forget.

Arrival and Waiting

Allow plenty of time for parking if coming by car as the Commissionaires are highly unlikely to let you park on site. Report to the reception desk and listen discreetly to make sure that the Receptionist lets the Director's office know that you have arrived. If the Receptionist is distracted by other phone calls and forgets, politely remind her. You may now have to wait a lengthy period. If you are lucky, you will be given a copy of the script, with the part marked for you to read. Having read the scenes involving the character for which you are being seen, you may have time to take in the whole script. You will form an impression of the worth of the story, be able to discuss your views, if asked by the Director, and you may find other suitable characters for which you would like to suggest yourself.

There will probably be other hopefuls waiting, but remind yourself that they are not necessarily up for the same part.

Type Casting

You will meet Actors who complain that their Agents are always putting them up for the same sort of part. Some have to accept that type casting – if they are lucky, policemen or crooks, (the two are interchangeable) – is a fact of television life; not just on account of their size, looks and physiognomy, but because they have to 'fit the bill' far more perfectly than in the Theatre. It is best for them to be philosophic, and hope that one day some wise Director will see how good they could be in a totally different part – it does happen.

Directors' Interviewing Techniques

At the B.B.C. the Receptionist will eventually ask you to go to a room number; listen carefully for directions – it is easy to get lost. The room will probably be untidy and small with three or four people talking on phones or typing, and with other people popping in and out – all very distracting. You are waved to a chair by the Director who is invariably using a phone. The room is overheated. When eventually the Director turns to you, you may be able to tell straight away if he is disappointed – your face has to fit his particular image of the character, but remember that he may never find that face and have to compromise. Once he gets talking to you, your personality may do the trick.

Directors vary in their interviewing techniques. Some will have a short chat, ask you to read, and then "we'll let you know". You can be out in five minutes. Others, will take twenty minutes or more. They like to file you on a bureaucratic form for future use, with all the details that they can get: "What stagework have you done recently?" "Have you done any commercials?" "What jobs did you do prior to Drama School?" (Do not be ashamed to mention that you worked in Woolworths or in a road gang. Most Directors will compliment you on broadening your insight of humanity). "Do you drive, ride, hang-glide, sing, dance, play a musical instrument, type; your height, age, colouring; where were you born and bred, what accents are you happy with; what languages do you speak, and to what standard?"

You may want to point out that most, if not all, of this information is in the C.V. that you sent with your photograph; but when you see the great pile of suggestions from Agents, Actors' letters and stacks of photographs on his desk, you may feel it prudent not to imply a criticism of his efficiency. He probably has read your C.V. but by asking these preliminary questions he has an opportunity to assess your personality.

When casting for later productions the Director will go through the forms of: "Those interviewed but not yet worked with." Although you may not get the part this time, there may be something in the future.

Abilities

Tell the Director anything and everything that might conceivably be useful; but do not lie about your abilities, particularly skills like driving, riding, swimming, tennis or typing. Contrary to the stories of the Hollywood Greats, it is not easy to learn overnight. If the part for which you are being considered requires a specific skill that you have not acquired, it is highly unlikely that you will have time to become proficient in it. If you are honest, the Director may be able to adjust the script to your capabilities.

Reading

Not all Directors will ask you to give a reading – many believe that it can be misleading rather than helpful. They have found that there are those who give a bad reading, but a relaxed, easy, natural screen performance; and those who read beautifully, but can be stiff and wooden when it comes to the actual rehearsals and performance. Should you be asked to read "on the spot", request time to look the part over in another room for a few minutes – try to be firm, as a rushed reading could lose you the job.

Introduction to Office Personnel

You will be introduced to the Production Team in the office; do not be dismissive or ignore them – they can be your allies. Once you have left it is highly likely that the Director will discuss you with them. If you get the part, these people are the ones with whom you will be in contact more than anyone else in the production. They may also be able to suggest you for future jobs.

The Production Manager (P.M.) is responsible for organisation and planning, finding locations, and taking the Director and Designer to approve them. He then organises permissions, catering, parking, etc. as well as the negotiation of *Facility Fees*. If filming in a built up area, he operates as a Public Relations Officer; liaising with the police and seeking the co-operation of residents and warning them about bright lights and noise. This is particularly important when on a *night shoot.*

During filming he will act as First Assistant to the Director, as well as ensuring the smooth running of the *shoot.*

On completion of filming he makes sure that everything is cleaned up and checks for damage.

In the Studio, he is in charge of the *Studio Floor* and becomes a diplomatic Sergeant Major; acting as a link between the Actors and the Director in the Production Gallery, keeping discipline and being responsible for the safety of Actors and Technical Crew.

Production Managers come from a variety of backgrounds, but most have been in the Theatre and are sympathetic to Actors.

The Production Assistant (P.A.) is a Secretary/Personal Assistant who, checks the availability of Actors with Agents, initiates bookings for production dates, fixes meetings between the Director and the servicing departments, checks continuity during filming and types the camera cards and camera script for the Studio side of the production.

In the Studio Gallery she times the programme, makes notes during recording of any retakes and calls the shots to the cameramen.

She keeps a file on every detail of the production, and is responsible for the paperwork that enables Actors to get their expenses.

The Assistant Floor Manager (A.F.M.) (B.B.C.); Stage Manager (S.M.) (I.T.V.) is responsible for: the *'Book'* – noting script changes, moves etc., props, your calls, Actors time sheets (overtime), marking up the Studio Set on the Rehearsal Room Floor and running the outside rehearsals. He becomes a Second Assistant Director during filming and is in charge of the first aid kit.

Most have a stage background. Some may be almost as new as you are to television. One A.F.M. on location filming, was sent to get the *'Chippy'* (carpenter), and eventually returned to report that: "All the chip shops were closed."

3 The Offer and Fee

Once the Director has made his choice of cast, he will check to see if the Producer has any objections. It is an unwise Director who does not listen to his Producer's opinion, but the final choice – both at I.T.V. Companies and the B.B.C. – is the Director's, as he is the one who will be working with the Actors.

Sometimes by the time an *offer* is made, the first choice is no longer available, and if a Director takes too long to make up his mind, he frequently ends up with his third or fourth choice. Bear this in mind when being interviewed; as Fay Compton said: "We are all thirteenth choice, dear."

After weeks of waiting, when you have at last given up hope, your Agent rings to say that they want you after all. Although he may not be entirely happy with the B.B.C's *offer* of a fee, he will probably tell you that he has done his best, and advise acceptance.

Should you be offered a good part and have no Agent, it is worth ringing *The Spotlight* offices and speaking to one of their Advisers for advice about the fee, and for suggestions of an Agent.

The B.B.C. is less flexible about fees than the Independent Companies, not just because the B.B.C. works to tighter budgets – which it does – but because the B.B.C. Bookers are restricted by much more rigid rules.

Whereas the Casting Director at the Independent Company negotiates with the Agent on the basis of an Actor's experience, size of role, and the number of days rehearsal, filming and studio, the B.B.C's system is largely based on the length of production, rather than on the size of role.

After weeks of waiting

An Actor, new from Drama School, who is in two episodes of a 50 minutes series, with only one very small scene in each episode, may do all his work in one day, on one film location. He will get the same two fees (Category II*) as another Actor, also straight from Drama School, whose work, in the same two episodes, involves a considerable number of scenes. These scenes may all be recorded in the Video Studio, requiring sixteen outside rehearsal and two recording days, over a period of twenty-eight days for both episodes, i.e. under the B.B.C. system an Actor working

*B.B.C. Programmes, Category I: 30 minutes and under; Category II: 31-60 minutes, Category III: 61-90 minutes, Category IV: over 90 minutes.

for one day, with one line in each episode, can get the same payment as another working for eighteen days on a large part in the same two episodes.

It is possible that the Actor with the larger role may be given a B.B.C. *Special High,* which amounts to a few pounds more than his fellow beginner. However, the B.B.C. is more likely to judge the situation on the grounds that the Actor doing one day's work is being overpaid, rather than that the one with eighteen day's work is being underpaid. You would be unwise to reject the part on 'a matter of principle regarding the fee.' In spite of the Director's vehement protestations that you are the one he must have for the part, he will end up having to find someone else, and you will have lost a chance to start establishing yourself.

A B.B.C. *Artists Index* keeps a card of your work and previous fees. These fees inch up over the years.

Paradoxically some excellent older Actors can find themselves losing jobs at the B.B.C. because their fees have climbed to a high level with past prestigious parts. If one of these Actors is offered a small but interesting role, which he would like to do for a basic fee, the Booker can only offer a *Special Low* – which will be a small amount below the fee reached when he was playing leads. The budget cannot afford him and, under this system, the Director and the Actor are both the losers.

There have also been cases of Actors who have not worked for the B.B.C. for some years, but who have done well in Independent television productions or Feature films, and who feel that they are now worth considerably more than what is, in their opinion, a derisory offer from the B.B.C. No agreement can be reached and the Director reluctantly has to cast his second choice who, because he has worked almost exclusively for the B.B.C., is more expensive than the first choice Actor would have been if he had been paid the fee that his Agent was asking. No such stumbling blocks exist with the Independent Companies.

4 Pre Production

Costume and Make-Up

Once you have been *booked* for the role, the Production Assistant will ring to check your address and phone number and, if you are involved in location work, Costume and Make-up will soon be in touch.

Disagreements can easily arise over personal taste, and both departments can appear wary and tough; having had trouble with fussy customers in the past.

Costume

Before seeing you, the Costume Designer will have had a discussion with the Director about mood, character and clothes, and with the Set Designer about colours and backgrounds. Both the Director and Costume Designer will want you to be as comfortable as possible, but bear in mind that the authenticity and the overall look are important. Uncomfortable period undergarments can be essential for posture and the look of a costume. However, if the costume seriously impedes your performance, it is to everyone's advantage to mention it. Do not suffer in silence, especially if the Costume Designer appears to have forgotten that modern toilet facilities are not designed for Dr Who monsters or crinolines.

Actors who provide their own costumes are not paid a fee, but the cost of cleaning or replacing damaged items is paid for by the Production Unit.

Different companies have different policies, and at the end of a production it is sometimes possible to buy, for a reasonable price, modern clothing that you have worn.

Make-up

The Supervisor will have talked to the Director about hair

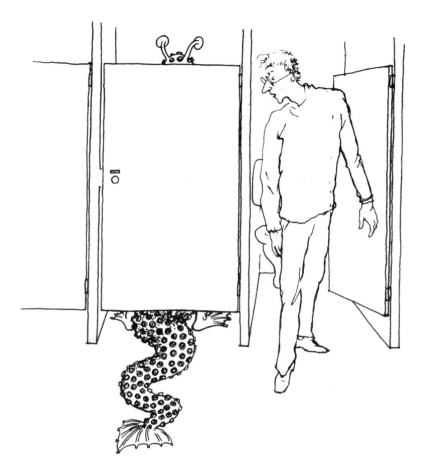

Who's in the loo?

and general style, and how an Actor's facial characteristics may effect make-up. You may find a *Hair Clause* in your contract. This is necessary because, in the past, cries of: "no one told me that I was going to have a short back and sides" have caused difficulties.

Use your common sense about skin tones and hair. If you have been cast as a pale poet, do not go off to southern Spain a week before filming, to return with a heavy bronze tan and a crew cut.

Trust the Make-up and Costume departments. They are all professionals, and can be helpful and sympathetic in a number of unexpected ways. During your first job, when you will be nervous, they will help you to get through, and can often give you useful information about who's who – and who's with whom – on the Unit.

Expenses

If costume or wig fittings are required, you will be given minimum expenses to cover travel by public transport. Should you be needed for fittings outside contracted hours, you will be paid a small fee. Keep receipts of any expenses necessarily incurred. For example, if, in order to get to rehearsals on time, you have to take a taxi from the Costumiers, ask for a receipt, the Production Manager will then refund you.

Advance payments of fares and expenses at a standard 24 hour rate, to cover hotel bills and a contribution towards the cost of breakfast, lunch and dinner, will be arranged before you go filming. If the cost of the only accommodation available is higher than the allowance, then the television company will settle the account.

When working on the location, meals are provided free.

Health

Try to avoid Medical or Dental appointments during your production dates; and whilst you are not expected to lead a cloistered life, try to avoid hazardous exercise. You will not be popular if you arrive for your first production day on crutches – or noticeably pregnant.

Foreign Filming

If going abroad check that your passport is still valid, and whether you need any injections – the production office or your doctor will be able to tell you which 'jabs' are advisable.

A cloistered life

5 Production Recording Methods

There are five basic alternative production methods of recording a programme.

All Film
Part Film, part Video Studio
All Video on location
Part location Video, part Studio Video
All Studio Video

Which method is chosen largely depends on the programme's content and budget allocation. For example, the All Film production generally gives the best product, but is often the most expensive.

6 Filming

Filming can be frightening for the beginner, but the frustrations for everyone of getting everything exactly right at exactly the right moment soon overcome the nerves.

It is inevitable that when the light is right to suit a previous shot, a sound will intrude and vice versa. When both Camera and Sound are eventually happy, Make-up will rush in with their powder puffs for your shiny nose, and by the time they have finished the sun has gone in again. Stoppages can continue for an apparent eternity, especially when animals are involved.

Especially when animals are involved

However, filming has the great advantage of the intimate communication that comes when a small team work closely together, the Actor is able to concentrate on small sections at a time, and there is always an element of spontaneity.

Lack of Rehearsal

Some Companies have an excellent system whereby, on a Film/Video project, you have a few days' rehearsal prior to filming, then go back to the rehearsal room before the Video Studio. Sometimes filming follows Studio work, but more often film inserts take place before the bulk of the programme is completed in the Studio. (It is for this reason that the Filming Section is placed before that on Rehearsals.)

You may be expected to do your final, most intimate scene on film, with a minimum of rehearsal. You will probably have discussions and line rehearsals in the hotel the night before, but even this may not happen if other Actors are unavailable, and you may meet your partner for the first time in front of the camera.

You will seldom be expected to perform without some form of rehearsal on location, however it is easy for these rehearsals to become orientated towards the camera and sound crews following the action.

The value of a quiet prior rehearsal on site, with only yourselves and the Director present is sometimes not possible for a variety of reasons: a tight schedule, the necessity to leave a location by a given time, rigging of lights, make-up, change of costumes etc.

The Schedule

This document is the work of the Production Manager and is the Unit's bible. Everyone, Artists and Staff, gets a copy – from Head of Department to the location vehicle drivers. It contains every conceivable piece of relevant information and is a diary of planned events – a day by day schedule of who, what, when and where – directions and maps to locations, property requirements, armourers and visual

You may meet for the first time in front of the camera

effects, parking, catering, loos, useful contacts, police, hospitals, technical requirements, arrivals and departures of personnel, train timetables, etc.

The average size of a film unit, not counting the Actors, will be thirty. As already stated, television is a team effort and one missing cog can throw everything into disorder. You are the major cogs. Time is money, and organisation is vital. The Production Manager will try to anticipate all problems, and cover for all eventualities, especially the weather. Thus you may well be called for Make-up and Costume at 6.00 am and then not work until after lunch, or even not at all that day. This is not necessarily bad organisation – it is playing safe, and after all you are being paid. You will see, at some time in your career, the annoyance of a crew hanging about, losing momentum and enthusiasm because 'X' was late for make-up and costume.

The shooting schedule is geared to the quickest, and most efficient, way of getting the filming completed. Obviously it is preferable to shoot in chronological order, and this is borne very much in mind for make-up, length of hair etc; but the schedule has to take into account the availability of locations, night shoots, police permission, availability of aircraft and so on. Only on exceptions is it worked out to the Actor's convenience, for example when he has to be finished by a certain date, or has an evening theatre performance. Even when you become a star, the emphasis will be on fitting you into the master plan rather than vice versa.

It is vital that you let the production team, particularly the Production Manager, know of any difficulties or uncertainties that you have, and make sure that they are always up to date on your whereabouts before and during filming, as schedules frequently have to be changed.

You may be in trouble if, when you receive the schedule, you whip through it, find that your scene is not listed until 3 o'clock on Monday and swan off on an incommunicado sailing weekend.

Hotels

If you prefer to travel to the location hotel in your own car, rather than by the train which will be met by a member of the production team, let them know. Absent Actors can cause the Production Manager sleepless nights and you may therefore prejudice your chances of future work.

Should you decide to go and stay with Auntie Flo twenty-five miles away, rather than with the Unit, it is true that you can pocket your expenses. However, give the Production Manager plenty of notice, or you will be booked into the hotel – do not cancel at the last minute.

There are many advantages to staying in the Unit Hotel. They will wake you for that early make-up/costume call. The risk of mishaps travelling to and fro is reduced, and you can keep in touch and be aware of any changes in the schedule. You can go through the next day's scenes with fellow Actors; and although it is not obligatory to stay up into the small hours, or prop up the bar, you have an opportunity to get to know the cast and crew.

The Film Crew

There is, generally speaking, more time for camaraderie with a film crew than with the larger number of studio personnel. You will find a variety of attitudes. There are those who will treat you gently and sympathetically; there are those who will regard you as a necessary evil – pawns in the grand design; there are cameramen who, when ready

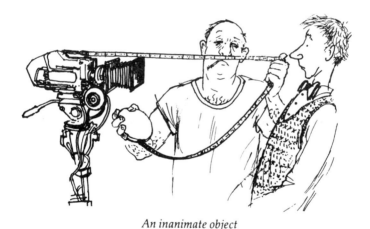

An inanimate object

for a take, will call out: "Rightyo bring on the comics", or will impolitely manhandle you onto your *mark*; there is the Assistant Cameraman who will run a measuring tape to your nose as if you were an inanimate object. But these characters are the exception rather than the rule; most technicians will help you in every possible way. In particular the good experienced Lighting Cameraman is very much aware of the importance of establishing a rapport with the Actors.

31

The Lighting Cameraman

Without the camera all is lost and the Cameraman is very much the king technician on location. The Director will have done a *Recce* of the locations with the Cameraman, and they will have discussed how best to shoot the scene; but plans often have to be changed. Rain necessitates umbrellas, the cars take up more room than expected, the Actors may have fresh ideas for moves, and then the Cameraman may see a better way of achieving the shot – making it visually more stimulating. These many aspects of the creative process must be co-ordinated with the Director, who is acting as chairperson, tactfully rejecting, gratefully accepting. It must be remembered that only the Director carries the overall picture in his mind – selecting where the emphasis should go, knowing how the adjacent scenes will look in comparison, and trying to avoid repetition. Trust that apparently silly or bizarre situations will piece together in the end.

When positions have been finalised after a rehearsal, and lighting is taking place, be unobtrusively available to stand in position; particularly for interiors. You will be of help to the Lighting Cameraman, see how it is done, and get used to your surroundings.

The Assistant Cameraman is responsible for the camera functioning, loading the film magazines, pulling focus and sometimes operating the camera. He often has the task of *marking* the shot with the clapperboard.

The Clapperboard or *Slate* has marked on it the name of the programme, the Director, the Cameraman, and a space for *Shot number and Take number*. For identification each shot is given a sequential number, and the take number is dependent on the number of times that shot is attempted; for example Shot 53 Take 4 may be identified in the continuity notes as: "Exterior, Barracks, Day, Scene 5, page 40 (in script). Tracking Close Up Tyson (Character). Take 1, N.G. (No Good) Sound-Aeroplane. Take 2 N.G. Artists fluff (hesitation during the dialogue), Take 3, N.G. Camera lost focus. Take 4....."

Do not be alarmed when you hear the Director call *Turn Over* – he is telling the Cameraman to start the camera. The Sound Recordist will then call out *speed*, meaning that the recorder is running, and that the Assistant can call out the shot number and take attempt – '53 take 4', before clapping down the hinged arm on top of the board. The point of impact is used by the Film Editor to synchronise sound and picture.

Reaction to "Action"

After the shot has been marked, wait for the *Action* cue. The Director may be waiting for a car to pass, or a member of the public to clear shot, and the Cameraman often has to adjust from lining up on the clapperboard, to the initial *frame* of the shot. As you hear the Assistant marking the shot, you will start to motivate yourself. Do not leap in so quickly when the Director calls *Action* that you overlap your dialogue with his word. It can mean a retake, you are not in a race and you can adversely affect your performance. Allow a moment before starting.

Most Directors will call *Action* quietly for gentle, sensitive scenes and loudly for scenes involving a lot of movement with crowds. Even though the Production Manager has called for silence before a shot is marked, there can be many reasons for minor delays before the start, and most Directors like to call *Action* loudly whenever possible, so that everyone knows that the shot is actually happening. The Director will call *cut* for the shot to finish.

The Grips is in charge of the camera equipment, with which he travels in the *Grips Van*. The *Tripod* (standard support for the camera), the *Jib Arm*, (for fluid movement sideways, as well as up and down), car mountings (the

33

camera can be clamped onto the bonnet or side of a car), *tracks* (mini railway), and the camera *Dolly*, which has a seat for the Cameraman and runs on the rails. He also carries equipment with exotic names like *A High Hat*, (a low mounting in the form of a vertical cylinder with a flange), and a *Bazooka*, (a taller adjustable vertical cylinder particularly useful in restricted areas, where a tripod would have too narrow a base).

Tracking Shots

When the camera *Dolly* has been put on the rails for a tracking shot, there may be a difference of opinion about speed of walking. The Director wants you to walk at a normal or fast speed, but the Cameraman wants you to walk slowly, so that the *Grips*, who is pushing the *Dolly* can keep up. A compromise will be reached. You may have to walk between the tracks, judging your steps, without looking down, to negotiate the cross sections; while your partner, with whom you have dialogue, walks not alongside, but a pace behind, in order that the camera can achieve a *tight two shot*. It will be awkward and uncomfortable, and you will feel that you look totally wrong. This may be your first experience of *It looks all right on camera* – the point being that you are not being shown full length, but that the camera is *framing* just below your shoulders, and your movement therefore looks natural.

When you are delivering dialogue from a static position you may be asked to move nearer to the Actor with whom you are playing the scene – to close the natural distance between you – in order to achieve a better *two shot*. Working at such close quarters may seem unrealistic, but: *It looks all right on camera.*

The Sound Recordist and His Assistant normally operate with a microphone on the end of a long pole or extendable boom. They often use hand held directional *Gun Mics*, but

34

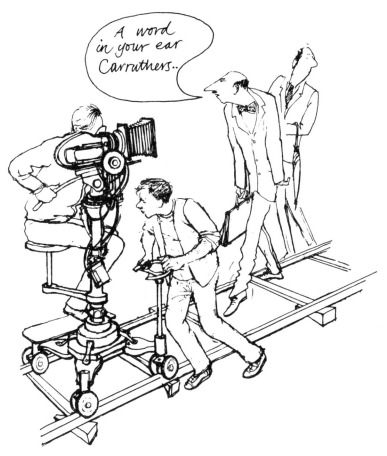

It looks alright on camera

are reluctant to work with *Radio Mics*, even though they may enjoy concealing them down the fronts of young actresses, and working out where to hide the battery. Radio Mics, once fixed and concealed, with the aid of the Costume department, may not give such good sound quality, but allow a lot more freedom for camera operation. Always remember to have your Radio Mic disconnected before your break, otherwise your intimate moments, both verbal and physical, may be widely broadcast.

The Sound Recordist will often want *more voice*. Normally he will first ask the Director, who will then approach you; but should the Recordist ask you direct, make sure, tactfully, that the Director approves. Directors are well aware that dialogue can sound theatrical if delivered too loudly.

A good Sound Recordist is often more perceptive of acting nuances than the Cameraman, and may well be consulted on this score by the Director.

The Lighting Crew usually consists of a Chargehand *(Gaffer)*, plus two or three electricians; all members of a strong Union, The E.E.T.P.U. (Electrical Electronic Telecommunication and Plumbing Union). At the B.B.C. they tend to be more involved with a production, and are sensibly scheduled to stay with it throughout the *Shoot*. At some I.T.V. Companies they are changed, almost daily, to accommodate weekly time sheets.

When the Gaffer shouts "Get out the Blondes and Redheads", do not expect a troupe of girls to appear; they are forms of lighting equipment; as are the suggestive *Double Broads*, *Bashers*, and *Brutes*.

The Designer is mainly concerned, during filming, to cover anachronisms. He may be asked to make Dundee look like Moscow with the aid of signs, cars, lorries and tons of salt. He may have to make a stretch of Welsh countryside look like an Afghan border post, with the use of huts and flags; convert a Dorset sandpit into a women's prison camp in Malaya or construct within it a Foreign Legion fort for 'Beau Geste'.

The art of the Designer is to create the right environment and atmosphere in which the production will take place. In order to do this he has to combine the skills of artist, architect, art historian and interior designer. He has to be able to present his ideas visually on paper, to deal with construction and scaffolding, and to know what the interior of an Elizabethan household or the inside of a space capsule should look like.

He has an Assistant to help him draw up the plans of the Studio Sets – normally up to eight depending on the size of the studio and the sets – as well as the script requirements. The Designer will supervise the construction of these sets, either within the company, or with outside contractors. He has to work within a budget and is allocated a certain number of *man hours* for construction. The Designer works in close conjunction with the Director, particularly in the early stages when they discuss preliminary sketches, points of emphasis, and how to use the budget, film locations and studio space to best effect. (If there is only a single two minute scene in one set, this will not have the same precedence as a set required for a number of scenes).

For interiors which are to be shot on film, the Designer may have to completely redress a room with period furniture. In conjunction with a *Properties Buyer* he will purchase certain items, but more often will hire furniture, cars, carriages, etc. from specialist companies. He also provides, with the Props Buyer, the *Action Props,* except the firearms, which the Actor is expected to operate: play around with the fire tongs in advance, try the scythe, push the pram and operate the typewriter before your scene. Mention when you are having difficulties and are worried that you are going to look inept. The Designer may be able to provide an alternative prop, or he may be able to help you to understand and operate the machinery. Do not say straight away, "It's impossible." He has gone to trouble and expense to find an authentic artefact and will be reluctant to see it discarded. If it is obvious to the Director that your performance is suffering, he will make the decision for you.

The Chippy (Carpenter) and Painter work to the Designer and will probably have done the major part of their work before you arrive on the Set.

An Authentic Artefact

The Propmen, (Film Operatives) in addition to handling props, also place any additional scenery and furniture. They make the beds, sometimes not too well, so check well in advance of the passionate love scene. They also help in a multitude of ways: pushing cars, holding *Dingle* (branches) in front of camera, helping control traffic, clearing paths, wiping rain off cars for continuity, etc.

The Visual Effects Designer is in charge of explosions, fires, windscreens shattering, bullets kicking up the earth or splintering doors as you run, breakaway furniture, trick props etc. If, after rehearsal, you are not absolutely sure what is supposed to happen or what you are to do, speak up.

The Armourer is in charge of guns, swords, knives, catapults, bows, crossbows and projectiles. If you are going to handle a weapon, find him well in advance. He will show you how to look right and cope with gun recoil. These days Actresses, as well as Actors, may be required to deal with all kinds of weaponry.

Try to avoid wasting the Unit's time by getting instruction during the actual *set up*. Do not sit back and wait if you feel that you can usefully employ yourself to save time later, but always check with the Production Manager or Assistant that you will not be intruding on the current shooting; and do not leave the Unit without clearance.

The Stuntman may be required to stand in for you during the more dangerous moments of a fight, or double for you falling off a horse or out of a car. Always be in a position, if possible, to note how his fall ends, so that you can, if necessary, duplicate the final movement.

The Stills Photographer will be there to take publicity pictures, either for the *Radio* or *T.V. Times*, or for use in the programme's promotion brochures. Because the shooting schedules are normally tight, the photographer has to take what he can during rehearsals, without holding up production. However, there will be times when you are not involved in a scene and the photographer would like to do some *stills* of you, with or without other Actors. Co-operate whenever possible; those shots will help sell the programme at home and abroad and may well mean a *Repeat* or *Residual* fee. You may also be able to buy a Close-up of yourself, that is suitable for use in *Spotlight*.

Cars

When driving always be safe; if a light on the bonnet is dazzling you or blocking your vision, say so. Make sure that you are well briefed before departure. You will have the Cameraman saying: "Favour me a bit more – no – your face, but keep your body hard against your door." The Sound Recordist, "More voice – can you get into top gear before you speak?". The Director, "Start the dialogue as we get to those columns, turn left – no sorry keep straight on." Wait for the Director's *Action* cue, and be aware that, for convenience, the clapper board may be put on to mark the end of the shot, not the beginning.

There have been occasions when an Actor has not tried his vehicle before a driving scene and then very much wished that he had. For example, a Jeep which you are to drive with three other Actors as passengers, is concealed round a corner waiting to enter a shell shattered village. The Assistant standing by you reports, via his *Walkie Talkie* to the Director, that you are in position with engine ticking over. A quarter of a mile away you hear a distant megaphone voice yell: "Start the fires and smoke, bodies into position, standby to crash the walls." After a minute of tension waiting for the fires to be at their peak, you hear *Action* from the Assistant's *Walkie Talkie*, and he waves you off. When you stall the jeep and cannot get it re-started, the whole shot will have to be prepared again. The set will not be the only thing to explode.

Protection of Costumes

One of the commoner sights during filming is the umbrella

Potential hazards to costumes

40

held aloft over the Actor, in case his *cossie* (costume) gets wet or marked. This always amuses the public, particularly when the costumes are of an extravagant bygone era. If fighting time, and the rain is not heavy, umbrellas are quickly taken out after the shot is *marked* and even more quickly replaced on *cut*.

Another hazard for the wardrobe department is the lunch or supper break when food is issued from trays in a cramped bus, where soup or gravy is easily spilt, or when Actors sit in a field which can also leave its marks. Sometimes Actors are issued with plastic overalls, but always be aware of any potential hazards to costumes.

Continuity is important on two counts: (a) for the technicalities of cutting the various shots together and (b) for mood when going from scene to scene, especially from film to studio.

It is the Production Assistant's job to note that you do your moves consistently, and she jots down at what point in the dialogue you turned your head, when you got up from the chair, when you took the cigarette from your mouth and with which hand, as well as noting the length of the cigarette.

Never be so worried about continuity that your performance suffers, but it is surprising how often good Actors can help; just because they are aware of these things.

There are times when the P.A. tells the Director that you did something differently, but he may accept the shot because he knows that he can edit round it; and there will be times when you disagree with the P.A., and the Director will tactfully make a decision. The instant polaroid picture is a considerable aid here, as it is to Make-up and other departments. Regarding mood: it can be difficult to remember continuity of thought from a previous scene. You have kissed passionately, with the Fire Brigade playing hoses on you, before rushing up steps, weeks or even months later, into a Studio Set, having been

41

showered by a watering can. Notes of adjacent scenes taken during filming will help you to recapture the mood.

Rushes

Every morning the rolls of film that have been shot the previous day are delivered to the Company's base by the laboratories that have developed them overnight. Known as *Rushes* or *Dailies* these first prints are viewed without sound, by the Film Operations Manager (F.O.M.), who reports any technical faults to the Cameraman by telephone. If there is no alternative way of piecing together the other shots to make a scene work, then a faulty *slate* will be retaken.

In the days of the big film studios, when Exteriors as well as Interiors were shot within the confines of the Studio *Lot*, *Rushes* would invariably be viewed by the Principals of the Cast, the Director, and the Cameraman. Nowadays *Rushes* are frequently transferred to a video cassette and delivered to the Unit on location, but most Directors do not encourage the Cast to be present at the viewing.

Sometimes the Film Editor's Assistant will have had time to *Sync Up* the sound to picture, but whether *Rushes* are viewed with sound or *mute*, they can be demoralising for Actors, who tend to see only their faults, and are often unaware of the sections which will be selected to make a scene. Many experienced Actors deliberately avoid seeing these misleading fragmented performances.

Location Behaviour

Always treat locations with respect. They are other people's property, so do not leave a mess behind you, and do not risk picking up valuables, – they may break, causing aggravation to the owner. This may seem obvious, but the behaviour of crowds encourages thoughtlessness.

Do not risk picking up valuables

7 The O.B. (Outside Broadcast) Unit

This production outfit operates in a similar way to filming, but with electronic video cameras – usually one or two operating together.

Comparison of Video to Film

Video has some advantages over film. The Director can see a scene as it happens on a *monitor* and is able to play back the shots immediately, to check that all is well. The editing of video programmes is quicker and cheaper than film, and does not involve the expense incurred with the laboratory skills of Negative Cutters and Colour Graders. The actual tape is cheaper than 'once only' film stock and it can be recorded over. When Exteriors have been shot on film to be edited to Video Studio Interiors, the change in picture quality is often evident. If Exteriors are shot on video and joined to Video Interiors, the presentation is smoother.

As the end product is cheaper and more quickly produced, Managements are increasingly keen to use video rather than film, but there are disadvantages. The Video Unit can be cumbersome with more vehicles in the travelling circus, and as yet the operation is not as sophisticated as filming. The camera cables, like umbilical cords, are restrictive and the camera picture is not as subtle as film. When the texture of the electronic picture is as good as film, then Producers and Directors will be more satisfied.

8 The Read Through

After filming, or the O.B., it is back to the calmer world of the rehearsal room and the *Read Through*. This may sensibly have taken place before filming, but more often happens on return from location work; particularly when the majority of the programme is to be recorded in the Studio.

When 75% of the programme content is already on film, the Director may think it pointless to have a *Read Through* of the remaining material; or if working to a tight rehearsal schedule, he may feel that he is wasting valuable rehearsal time. The long running twice weekly Serials seldom have time for a *Read Through*. However, if there is one, it is an occasion when you will meet other members of the cast who have not been on location, or those who have not worked on the same days as yourself, and you may be introduced to the Author and Script Editor for the first time.

The Author

With television it is generally accepted that the priorities are: script, casting and production. If you have a good script, and it is well cast, then the production should be comparatively easy; and this is nearly always the case. Even though a good cast and production can gloss over a bad script; more often the product is unsatisfactory.

It therefore follows that the Author is of great importance, nevertheless he is often not treated with the respect that is his due. As a customary courtesy he is invited to the *Read Through*; thereafter you may never see him. This may be because he does not want to be present while his script is being mangled, or that he is busy on another project, or has not been asked to appear, as he is known as an Author

When the Director has missed the point

who can give the Director and Actors a difficult time. But, most Authors are very much aware of the value of *production time* and of when it is politic to let a minor point go.

They can be amenable, when reasons are given for script changes and improvements. There will be times when they can indicate that the Actor and Director have missed the point and, not surprisingly, they can often improve the Actor's or the Director's alteration of their script.

Should you want to have a personal chat with the Author, it is tactful to approach the Director first. Most Authors will be delighted if you want to discuss your character.

If he is around during Filming, Rehearsal or the Studio and does not approach you, it is probably not because he thinks that you are lousy, but because he feels obliged to keep a back seat. If you genuinely like the script, do not be afraid to go up and tell him so, it is not sycophantic, and nearly everybody thrives on praise.

When most of the programme content is to be recorded in the Studio, the Author, if available, should come, on his own, to an outside rehearsal *Run Through* and then sit down for a discussion with Cast and Director. These meetings are nearly always constructive and by no means one sided.

The Script Editor

The Script, or Story, Editor is often instrumental in finding and suggesting Writers to the Producer. In a Series, where there will be many Writers, he makes sure of the continuity of characters, tries to look after the Author's interests and sometimes writes additional material, when it is required at short notice. He also checks, as far as is possible, that names of people and firms in the script do not equate with reality. Any alterations of the script in rehearsal go to the Script Editor rather than the Writer. In most Independent Companies there are no Script Editors – the Producer encompasses their brief, with the help of a Researcher.

Queries and Comments

If you have not been on location and this is your first production day, you should still have been sent a script well in advance. Should the script not arrive, it may have got lost in the post; or it may be your fault because you have not informed the Production Office of a change of address. If no script has arrived a week before the *Read Through*, check with the Production Office.

Get to the Rehearsal Room early in order to see the Director with any queries that you think can be solved before the *Read Through*. "Is that a misprint? If not, then I cannot understand what it means." You may want to know how to pronounce some *Bon Mot*, or be worried about sounding foolish for other reasons. As the start time approaches the Director will probably be deep in conversation with the Producer, or busy greeting the Stars as they arrive. Before the start, the Director will introduce everyone and say a few words. Some Directors prefer queries and comments that arise during the Reading to wait until the end, so that everyone gets an overall feel of the script, and the production team can get a very approximate idea of the length of the programme, but others prefer queries to be raised as they occur, while they are fresh in everyone's minds.

Do not give your *all* during the Read, but do not be so laconic that you find yourself replaced.

After the *Read Through* the Author is, or should be, asked by the Director if he has any comments, then the Producer and Director may make some remarks and the Script Editor may point out an error in the script that has come to light during the Reading. With luck someone in the Cast will raise a point which leads to other questions. As the Author may never be seen again, do not hesitate to ask for clarification.

Costume Appointments
Before, or after, the Read Through, or on the first day of Rehearsal, Costume and Make-up may be waiting to see you, if you have not already met, in order to fix appointments to shop or fit. They may have checked with the production team the times that you are available from rehearsal, but make absolutely sure with the A.F.M. or S.M., who will be aware of any alterations to the schedule. You may be expected to be available in the evenings, after rehearsal, for costume fittings.

9 Rehearsals

Different Directors have different methods of rehearsal, but be punctual and bring a pencil.

Call Sheet

Most Directors will have worked out a call sheet of the scenes that they want to work on in any given day, so that Actors are not kept hanging about. However, this does not always happen – you may be called 'just in case', and you may find that you do not work that day. Frustrating, but remember that you are under contract.

Never leave at the end of your day's rehearsal without checking your next day's call with the A.F.M. If you cannot be contacted at your usual number for any later change of call, let the A.F.M. know your movements: "I'm going to the theatre and won't be back till late, if there's any change ring before I go for my run at eight tomorrow morning – if I'm not in try......"

Character Motivation

When the time comes for you to rehearse, you may be expected to wade into a scene with a minimum, if any, of *character motivation* discussion. Some productions have plenty of time to rehearse and experiment, but most work to a tight schedule. At your interview the Director will have given you an idea of how he sees the character, and he now waits to see what you will present.

You have been cast because the Director sees you in that particular role. He believes that you can call on certain qualities – voice, looks, physique, presence, stillness, etc., to convey that person. It is not like working in a Repertory Company where you will play many and varied parts,

49

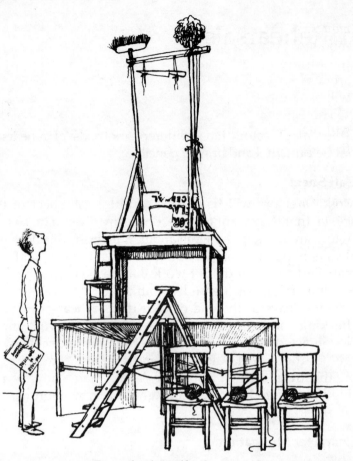

Do not be alarmed by the props

young and old. The Director will expect you to find your *character* comparatively early. He should always be receptive to ideas, so do not hesitate to contribute, and do not be afraid to do too much – it is easier to bring a peformance down rather than up.

Blocking the Moves

The Director will show you the layout of the Set, marked in coloured tape on the floor, before starting to *Block the moves.* With luck he will be able to show you a Designer's model, which will help considerably. Do not be alarmed by the furniture or props used in the rehearsal room, which are a very rough approximation to those with which you will be working in the Studio Set.

The Director may have definite ideas about your *moves.* Although they may seem alien to you, try them his way first, then maybe proffer your suggestion.

When not working on your scenes, most Directors will be happy for you to sit in a corner of the rehearsal room and watch. You can learn a great deal from observing experienced Actors.

Comments from the Regulars

Most of you will probably start with a small part in an unprestigious soap opera or series. Be wary of the *Regulars* who say, "Bloody awful script", or "I'm only doing it for the money". Judge for yourself. Sometimes a script that seems lacklustre at the Read Through can develop in rehearsal and recording into something exciting and stimulating. A television script very much involves visual descriptions and although the dialogue may be more important than the picture, images are invariably more potent than the spoken word.

Many well made American series are compulsive viewing, in spite of banal dialogue.

Size of Shot and Points of Emphasis

At a latish stage in rehearsal, the Director may tell you when the camera is going to be close on you, so that you can keep your performance subtle, or when on a wide angle so that you can give more. If he does not tell you his shots, you can often guess by the closeness and intensity of his stare in rehearsals.

The Director selects his points of emphasis – which character should be given priority on the screen at a given moment, when to see the eyes in *close up*, or the action in wide shot etc. – from the intentions of the script, and during rehearsal when he sees the Actor's contribution.

The question of whether it is wise to know how a Director is shooting a scene is debatable. Some Actors prefer not to know, in case by consciously tuning their performance they come across theatrically. Others will tell you that there have been times when they have given a marvellously intense burning look which went for nothing in a wide shot, and if they had realised what was happening they would have conveyed their thought with a gesture.

The Camera Never Lies and Mannerisms

Although the saying, "the camera never lies" may seem far fetched, it is very near the truth. Your performance should come from *within*; superficiality is soon spotted. Think it don't *Act* it; false unnatural gestures are fatal. Instinct, which fosters inspiration, is one of the most important weapons in your armoury and analysis one of the most dangerous.

When you first read a script you will naturally analyse the character you are to play, and prior to, and during, rehearsals there is inevitably, and rightly, a certain amount of exploration and experimentation with the role. However, there can come a stage when the more you analyse, dissect and clutter your brain, the less you feel, and consequently the more inhibited and less natural, or spontaneous, your performance will appear. All forms of mannerism are exaggerated, particularly in *close up* – the most important shot in television. Telling moments are often effectively conveyed by reaction *close ups*. You may have no dialogue in a scene, but your reaction can often say far more to an audience than a long speech.

Over or Under Rehearsing

The Director has to judge the difficult balance between over and under rehearsing; bringing on the *slow burner* and keeping fresh the Actor who is *there* straight away. Actors vary in their techniques and should approach the job in the way that is most natural to them, but must always take into account the amount of time allocated for rehearsal, and allow for the fact that some Directors deliberately under-rehearse to achieve more spontaneity.

You may be disheartened by some Directors who never say anything to you. They are just as likely to be of the breed who believe in not interfering if you are *on course,* as the ones who are preoccupied with *timings* – each programme has to fit a timed *slot* – or camera angles.

Technical Motivation for Cutting Between Shots

The Director will try not to bother you with technicalities unless he has to, but you will probably be asked to turn your head on a given line to motivate a camera cut to another Actor, or to lean forward in your chair on a certain line.

In the Studio you may be asked to contort – to put the weight on your left foot and lean forward – or to *cheat* your eyeline, so that you are not looking directly at your partner, but more to camera, or, when you get up from a chair, to rise vertically, so that you come up cleanly into close up or do not *mask* another Actor.

Part of your art is to make the unnatural look natural.

Script Cuts and Additions

During the last day or two of rehearsals, in particular for Series or Serials, you may be told that the script is over or under running. The Director is generally happier if it is over running, because it means that he can tighten up the pace of the programme; in which case your favourite dialogue, or even scene, may be cut. You may object strongly and find reasons why your sections are vital to the plot, and you may of course be right. However, the Director and Script Editor, or Producer, have carefully consulted, and will have the important points of the story very much in

The art of making the unnatural look natural

mind. By all means voice your objections, but know when to accept a necessity gracefully.

Understandably, Actors tend to see a production solely from their character's point of view – this can be misleading. Remember that it is the parts that make up the whole.

Judi Dench tells an anecdote about her daughter who, when a child, took the part of the Innkeeper's wife in an infant school nativity play. When asked by a friend what the play was about she said: "It's about this Innkeeper's wife....."

When under running, additional material will be written for existing scenes or even new scenes incorporated. More often than not this *padding* adds nothing of importance to the story, but it can elucidate points and give an Actor in a minor role more of a chance to shine.

Getting Time Off For Interviews

Some Directors will not let you go to interviews during their rehearsal time, but others will try to help, and be delighted that there is a possibility of more work for you. Obviously your Agent will try to fix an appointment before or after the production's scheduled rehearsal time, but this is seldom possible – though there are productions when the Director will only rehearse a long morning, or will start rehearsals after lunch.

Approach the A.F.M. first with your problem; he will know of any change of scheduled rehearsal times and when is the safest time to ask for leave of absence. When approaching the Director, if possible make sure that the A.F.M. is there, so that he will be aware of any change in the rehearsal schedule, can back you up, and can hear the decision.

Sometimes the A.F.M. will do the asking for you, so that he can explain how it will effect other Actors' calls, and when it would be best for you to go.

10 The Technical Run-Through

This will take place in the rehearsal room a day or two prior to the Studio date. The Technical crew see the script performed in recording order – seldom in story order, because once the cameras and sound booms are in one part of the Studio, covering a given Set, it is more economical of time to keep them there, rather than have them dodging back and forth between scenes. In the days of live drama this called for considerable planning in the movement of equipment during transmission.

The Production Planning Meeting

At a meeting with servicing personnel, which takes place before rehearsals, the Director explains his aims – the mood and atmosphere that he would like to achieve, his basic intentions in the way of shots, what camera mountings he may need to obtain these shots, and in what order he intends to record the programme. At this stage Make up and Costume may point out the time required for changes and suggest an adjustment in the *Running Order*. The Lighting and Sound Supervisors try to foresee any problems with the Sets which, when possible, are presented in model form, and have been drawn up by the Designer on a master plan of the Studio, leaving enough space to accommodate the technical equipment and crews.

As a result of this planning meeting – when the various experts contribute their ideas and suggestions – adjustments and compromises are often made. A team effort with all contributions, artistic or mechanical, being orchestrated by the Director.

The Camera Plan

During rehearsals the Director has worked out, on the large Studio master plan, from which points he wants his cameras to operate. A camera may have twenty or more different positions during recording; these are noted alphabetically on the plan (eg Camera Three's positions will be noted as: 3A, 3B, 3C etc).

The cameramen are given cards marked with the shots that they are required to take from the given positions on the plan. All these shots and camera moves are noted in the camera script which is distributed to all studio personnel, and which incorporates all the necessary information for a smooth Studio operation.

A Depressing First Audience

At the Technical Run do not be dismayed that the Technicians are nearly all looking at their plans or *Running Orders*, and not at you. They will be jotting down the moves and looking for the problems that can be solved before going into the Studio. They are your first audience and they may depress you by hardly reacting. However, remember that they are not there to sit back and enjoy a performance but are concentrating on their particular tasks.

The Lighting Supervisor has the task of lighting for more than one camera at a time – often four cameras will be intercutting shots from various angles. Apart from mood and subtle lighting of the performers in their various positions, he has to work in close conjunction with the Sound Supervisor to avoid shadows from the sound booms. Under his command he has a Lighting Crew and a Vision Controller, who balances the pictures from the different cameras, to make sure that there is no harsh jump in picture quality. He also has the difficult job of matching the film and studio pictures.

57

Your first audience

The Technical Operations Manager (T.O.M.) ensures that all the necessary equipment arrives in the Studio, and that it all functions properly. He liaises with unseen departments, such as *Telecine* who feed in the edited film, and *VT*, the Video Unit who record the Studio output. He also liaises with the Director and Producer on Union rules and, if necessary, initiates any request for Technicians' overtime.

The Sound Supervisor not only controls the operation and movement of the booms, stand microphones and sound apparatus in the Studio, through his Assistants on the

Studio floor, but also has an Operator in his control room feeding in any additional sound effects, which he balances with the dialogue.

The Scene Supervisor ensures, together with the Designer and Production Manager, that the scenery is properly placed, safe and ready for the start of Studio rehearsals. (Nevertheless there are nearly always minor adjustments to be made during rehearsals, and your dialogue may well have to compete with background banging). The Scene Supervisor has a Scene Crew who can, if necessary, move the scenery in and out – walls are swung on hinges, *camera traps* opened and closed during the *Action*. A scene is often shot twice from different angles – which can involve removal or insertion of walls. There are also times when Sets are double banked: the scenes in one Set are completed, and then this Set is removed to reveal another one behind. A good and willing Crew can save considerable time in the studio.

The Property Man who works to the A.F.M. or S.M., will look after cigarettes, drinks, food, flowers, pens, paper, chalk, etc. If waiting, in the Studio, for your scene to be rehearsed, check items such as the filing-cabinet drawer from which you have to take a file; it may not open or it may be empty. If the A.F.M. is not available, point out the problem to the Props man.

The Vision Mixer operates in the *Studio Gallery*, alongside the Director, and works from the camera script which indicates where to intercut between cameras at any given point in the dialogue or action. The Vision Mixer often suggests different points of emphasis, but it is vital that all the relevant Technical Crew know of any changes – for example if going from a close shot to a medium shot, the sound boom will be *skied* after a given word or move. Sometimes an Actor will inadvertently transpose dialogue, which, although it still makes absolute sense and has not thrown his fellow Actor, may have thrown the intercutting of the cameras. The Vision Mixer will try to cover every nuance in the performances, sometimes deliberately delaying a fraction to catch a look or cutting quickly to get a reaction. The Director may well have marked these points on the camera script, but the Vision Mixer's judgement is vital.

11 The Producer's Run-Through

This will normally take place after the Technical Run, but not necessarily on the same day. It is in story order with Producer, Script Editor and, hopefully, Author present.

On completion of the *Run*, the Cast go for a coffee break, while a general discussion takes place – the observations of three or four people trying to look objectively and make improvements.

Is the intention of the script clear? Can performances be improved? Is the pacing right? etc., Notes are then given to the Cast by the Director and any adjustments made.

12 The Studio

Prior Walk Through

When the Studios are not under pressure, it is sometimes possible for the Scene Crews to put up the scenery and place the furniture in position by the day prior to the first Studio day. The Actors then have the useful advantage of a *walk through*, with no Studio machinery involved, but with key Technicians sometimes present. They can adjust to the real furniture, ask for chairs to be made higher (either with blocks or cushions), point out any moves that will not now work, and generally get the feel of the Sets; as well as save valuable production time the next day.

Costume and Make-up for Studio Rehearsal

At the Companies where the practice is to Rehearse/Record you will be called in early for Costume and Make-up. At the B.B.C. you are usually asked to be in costume during the *plotting*, but not necessarily to be made up, except possibly when wigs are involved. Not only does this help you to sort out any problems before recording, but it gives the Designers a chance to check colours etc.

In particular, always rehearse with hats and caps. There have been occasions when the surprise appearance and size of a hat has meant that time-wasting adjustments to lighting and camera shots have had to be made during the recording time.

Relationship with the Studio Technical Crew

Because of the large number of personnel, and the comparatively short time spent in the Studio, it can be difficult for Actors and Crew to strike up a rapport. If the Camera,

The sudden appearance of a hat

Sound and Scene Crews are introduced, there can be too many names to be remembered. However, on a long running Series or Serial, names and faces become familiar, and a good working relationship can be established. In particular try to remember the cameramen's names as they are the technicians with whom you will be in most contact. Some thoughtfully tape their names on the front of the camera. Although television filming is by no means leisurely, you will be more aware of the lack of time in the Studio and this can create a tense atmosphere, but you will generally find the Crews helpful, cheerful, patient and professional.

The Studio Machinery

On entering a Television Studio for the first time most people's immediate reaction is surprise at the complexity and multitude of lighting *Hoists, Barrels* and lamps suspended from the *Grid* high in the ceiling. Some are surprised at the size of the electronic cameras which are, at present, considerably larger and more obtrusive than the film camera, particularly when the normal complement of five are operative. They then notice the sound boom platforms, three or four to a Studio, which can be pushed with an Operator standing four feet off the ground, and which take up space. Even the largest Studio can appear cramped when all the scenery is up, and all the equipment with its trailing cables has been wheeled in. It is easy for Technicians to momentarily forget that the Actors are more important than the machinery.

Plotting the Moves

How can Actors rehearse with so much activity going on? Scenery being moved in their eyeline. Red lights winking on the cameras – on top of each electronic camera a red, numbered, perspex light is illuminated to indicate when that camera is *live*. Actors being referred to rather like puppets with an unseen manipulator. Come the recording, the Actors will be the focus of attention, but in the early stages of the Studio everyone's main concern is technically *plotting* the moves, so do not give your full performance at this stage.

Most Directors do a rough plot of a scene on the Studio Floor and then disappear to the *Gallery* where they can see each camera's output, for a *stagger through*. When things grind to a halt because of some snag, do not rush in with: "Would it help if....", wait – the Director has probably got six voices going at him already. You can sense the moment when to make your brilliant suggestion via the Production Manager, who is now acting as Floor Manager.

Studio Discipline

As always time is at a premium and waiting while missing Artists are located is costly as well as annoying. Be aware of progress in the Studio. Listen on the dressing room tannoy,

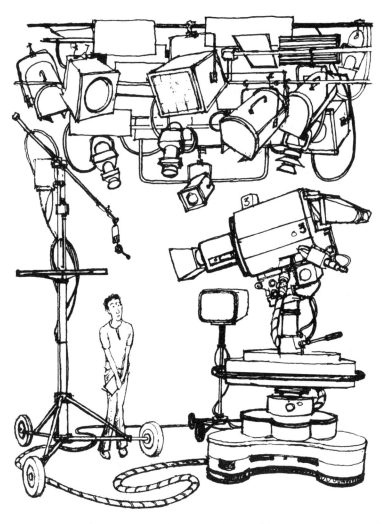

Actors are more important than machinery

which relays the Studio output. Anticipate your call. If you are in Make-up or Costume, let them know that your scene is coming up. Arrive on the Set in good time and let the Floor Assistant, who is responsible for getting Artists to the Set, see that you are present. You can either watch quietly from a distance or wait in your Set. When and where possible, check furniture, doors and props, etc., before the cameras and sound booms arrive at the Set.

Panics often ensue when Actors visit one another's dressing rooms and do not let production know where they are.

When a scene in which you are involved is stopped by a "Hold It" from the Floor Manager, do not start gossiping. The microphone above your head is *live*; an unnecessary babble of voices is very irritating to the *Gallery* and adds to the confusion.

Marks

Because positions are critical, you will be given *marks* on the floor to walk to; but if you can get into position relative to the furniture, do so and say so – it saves you looking down. When rehearsals are taking place elsewhere take the opportunity to perfect *getting onto your marks*, so that you are confident enough to move without worrying or looking down. This is best done by counting the paces required.

During the Studio *plotting*, furniture positions will be carefully marked on the floor or carpets. Chairs may be moved to as many as four sets of marks to accommodate different shots in different scenes. It is therefore vital that you do not move the furniture, other than is required during the action. You may be eager to help the production by moving your chair when adjustments are being made during the *plotting*, but be careful; in most Studios the Unions are very sensitive about who does what.

When the position of objects on tables, such as lamps or photographs are critical for the shots, these may also be *marked*. If you are showing a colleague that interesting photograph of your character as a child, replace it exactly as it was.

Different Rehearsal/Recording Methods

At the B.B.C. it is normal practice to plot and rehearse all scenes, and then record them en bloc.

An average 50 minute Episode in a B.B.C. series will be allocated three day's filming, during which approximately twelve minutes of programme time will be achieved. The remaining material will be covered in two Studio days.

Day 1: 1400-2200 hours *Day 2:* 1030-2200 hours, with the Recording, during which the film inserts will be played in, taking place between 1900-2200 hours. Because of Child Actors, large numbers of Sets, Crowd Artists or scene changes, prerecording of some scenes may take place earlier.

Independent Companies usually rehearse a scene and then record it. This can take some of the pressure and tension off the Actors; though some prefer to keep the adrenalin going and feel that they can achieve better performances and variation of pace over a concentrated recording period.

13 The Studio Recording

The Clock and Countdown

The start of Recording can be a prolonged agony for Actors, but try not to get yourself unnecessarily tensed up. The Production Gallery ask the hidden Video Recordist to run his machines, the Floor Manager gets everyone on *standby* and the Gallery tells the Floor Manager to *start the clock*. (This is lined up in front of a camera and is part of a board with programme details chalked on it). The Floor Manager counts down the last ten seconds of what can be a minute run up, and then *cues* the action.

The Floor Manager's Cue

It is normal to cue the Studio action with a silent hand movement. Floor Managers vary in their sensitivity – some do not look at you and will give a broad, violent, nervous, jerky movement when you are about to embark on a gentle scene. Other sensibly catch your eye and give an affirmative gentle nod and hand movement. If while *plotting* you are uncertain from which point you are going to get your cue during recording, ask the Floor Manager to clarify the situation; it will save time later and help to keep your mind at ease.

The Verbal Ident

After the recording is stopped, and when the next scene is ready to go, the Floor Manager gets the go ahead from the Gallery and then verbally *Idents* the scene, before cueing the Action: "Scene 31 take 1", or "Shot 231 onwards take 1", or "Insert for scene 31." All scenes, or inserts after the initial clock, are marked verbally. Some Independent Companies insist on putting a board in front of a camera and counting down the last ten seconds for every take, retake or insert. This can be irritating to even the most experienced actors.

Retakes

Most retakes are for frustrating technicalities, but regard them as another chance. If there are a number of *takes* then the Director can select from them when piecing the programme together. He will be looking at all the *takes* on his V.H.S. Cassette – looking for best performance and best technical shots. (As an aid for the Director, all studio output is recorded on a Video Cassette Recorder with a continuous *Time Code* printed in the bottom of frame).

If you feel that you have done a bad take, but it seems that the scene will not be retaken, try to catch the other Actors' eyes – they may well feel the same. The Floor Manager can ask for a *Take for the Actors;* but trust the Director's judgement.

Film Inserts

You may see the film inserts being played on the Studio Monitor and think, in your excited state of mind, that your Studio performance does not match. The Director has worked with the Film Editor putting the sequences together and would have said something in outside rehearsal if the two performances were noticeably different.

Studio Clearance

Finally, when you have completed your scene or scenes, do not leave the Studio building until you have had a definite clearance from the Floor Manager. Having completed the programme, the Director may want to go back and do retakes or insert shots, if he has enough recording time left.

14 Conclusion

The content of a television programme, although more important than its technical presentation is nevertheless largely dependent on, and conditioned by its presentation.

Because they care, every Department tends to think that its contribution is the most vital to the production. In spite of encouraging everyone to strive for technical perfection, the Director will always be aware that it is your face on the screen, allied to your joint interpretation of the script, that is the most important single factor.

After reading of some of the difficulties that can be encountered in television production, you may be apprehensive about working in such a demanding medium. Overcome your qualms. You will find that, although challenging, television can be enjoyable and rewarding. You will probably agree with Noel Coward that "Television is for being on, not for looking at."

Television is for being on not for looking at

Terminology

Production terminology and abbreviations can be confusing. You will be told, "We are going to do your *M.S.* and then your *C.U.*" – Medium shot (waist up), and Close Up (Head and Shoulders). You may be asked for more *d.bs* – decibels (more voice); or hear. "Don't worry Make-up, he's *o.v.*" – out of vision; or after one of your film takes be disconcerted to hear the Sound Recordist say to the Director, "well it wasn't marvellous, but you should be able to sort it out on the *dub*, can I do my *atmos track* now?" When cutting between shots – particularly during the filming of exteriors – the noise background can be different. A general atmosphere track and sound effects, like distant church bells, can be laid with the dialogue track, during the sound dubbing process, to make a smooth unobtrusive final sound-track.

Glossary

Listed below are some of the terms, abbreviations and phrases that you may hear.

AATON, a 16mm film camera.

A/B, as before – used in connection with a camera shot that is repeated exactly as before.

A.B.S., Association of Broadcasting Staff. Represents all categories of staff at the B.B.C. Recently amalgamated into the B.E.T.A (q.v.)

ACTION, 1. the content of a scene. 2. The cue given by the Director or Floor Manager to commence performance.

ACTION PROPS, objects used or handled by Actors.

A.C.T.T., Association of Cinematographic Television and Allied Technicians, the Union to which Technicians have to belong in order to work for Independent Companies.

A.F.M., Assistant Floor Manager (B.B.C.)

AMBIENT LIGHT, light surrounding the subject – generally of a soft low contrast quality.

ANGENIEUX, a lens manufacturer.

ANSWER PRINT, the first graded print of the edited film – adjustments to colour may be required.

ANTI FLARE, a solution used to spray down surfaces which are too reflective – particularly glass.

ARRI, Arriflex. A 16mm film camera. The most common in use for Television filming.

ARRILITE, a lightweight multi beam lighting unit.

ARTIST'S INDEX, a confidential department who keep a record of Actors, their programmes, fees and Agents.

ASPECT RATIO, proportion of picture width to height. e.g. 4 to 3 for Television.

ATMOS, a sound atmosphere track recorded to iron out the discrepancies in background noise.

BABY LEGS, a small tripod for low angle film shots.

B/G, Background.

BACK LIGHT, light directed towards camera from behind the subject. Also called 'Rim-light'.

B.A.F.T.A, British Academy of Film and Television Arts.

B.C.U, big close up – cutting above the eyes and on the chin.

B.E.T.A. Broadcasting Entertainment Trades Alliance

B.P., Back projection. Background film is projected onto a screen from behind, with the Actors in front. The illusion of travelling can be given by placing a static car in front of a B.P. Screen.

BANANA, "do a banana" – walk in a small curve from A to B so that you enter the shot at the right time in the right place, and/or do not mask another Actor.

BARNEY, a cover used to reduce camera noise when a blimp (q.v.) is not usable. This can be necessary when certain equipment is attached to the camera.

BARN DOOR, an adjustable framework of metal flaps fitted to a light to control the beam.

BARREL, a hanging bar for lights in the Studio.

BASHER, a small light used in filming.

BATTEN, a length of wood used for strengthening scenery.

BAZOOKA, an alternative to a film camera's tripod, consisting of a three-armed metal base, into which are fitted vertical sections of metal tubing, approximately the diameter of a drain pipe, to obtain varying heights. Useful in a confined corner and when the camera has to follow action over a wide arc.

BLIMP, the sound-proof covering for a film camera.

BLOCKING, the first rehearsal of a scene, when moves are worked out. Can also describe the first camera rehearsal.

BLONDE, a 2kw lightweight lamp.

BLOW DOWN, to spray scenery or costume with paint or dye, in order to reduce colour, and to age artificially.

BOOK, 1. The Assistant Floor Manager's or Stage Manager's script with all the Actors moves and script changes noted. 2. To engage an Artist for a role.

BOOM, a telescopic arm which holds the microphone close to the Actors, but out of shot. It can be hand held or mounted on a moveable platform.

BROAD, soft source of incandescent light.

BRUTE, a very large carbon arc lamp.

BUNGIE, a length of thick rubber tied to the end of a rope, to soften the jerk when a Stuntman falls.

CABLE BASHER: a junior Studio Cameraman, who makes sure that there is sufficient cable for a camera to achieve its shots, and that the cable is clear of obstacles.

CAMERA CARDS, the cards attached to a Studio Camera giving information about all the planned shots.

CAMERA TRAP, an opening frame, hinged or sliding, in a Studio Set, for a camera to shoot through – usually concealed to look like a picture or panelling.

CAM-RAIL, a lightweight monorail for tracking film or video cameras.

CANS, headphones.

CHAPMAN NIKE, a large camera crane with four operators.

CHEAT, a legitimate deception to achieve a desired result i.e. an Actor in Close Up can cheat his eyeline to another Actor out of vision, in order to achieve more face to camera.

CHERRY PICKER, a mobile hoist used as a camera platform for high shots. One member of a production team heard the Director say: "This is the day that we need the Cherry Picker" and promptly went to book a non-speaking Artist.

CHIPPY, carpenter.

CHUCK WAGON, Catering Van.

CLAPPERBOARD, used for shot, scene and take numbering. A hinged arm bangs down on the board so that the sound and picture can be synchronised for editing.

CLIP, piece of film taken out of a sequence.

C.U, close up – head and shoulders shot.

C.S.O, colour separation overlay. An electronic process whereby a person or object appearing in front of a blue or yellow Studio background can be superimposed over a separate source of film, video, photograph or caption.

CRAB, move the camera sideways.

CREEPER, a low angled mobile studio camera platform.

CRIB CARDS, see camera cards.

CROSSING THE LINE (See Diagram), intercutting camera shots should always be taken from the same side of an imaginary line drawn between Actors in a scene; otherwise a disorientating effect will be achieved. If this is applied to a travelling car the effect can be even more confusing, as it will appear to have suddenly reversed direction.

CROWD ARTISTS, see EXTRAS.

CUE, 1. a starting signal that can be given by a gesture, a light or verbally. 2. The action or speech which signals the start of

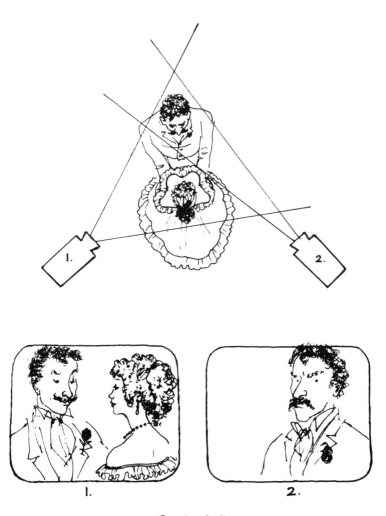

Crossing the line

action or speech of another Actor.

CUT: 1. the Director's instruction to a Camerman to stop the
camera at the end of a take. 2. To delete a word or passage from
a script. 3. To change from one shot to another.

CUTTING COPY, the working copy of assembled film which may
well show the chinagraph pencil marks, cellotape joins etc,
that will have been made while working to get the best result.

DEAD, 1. sound that does not reverberate. 2. Scenery or props that are finished with. 3. The point to which scenery is raised or lowered to be in a correct position.

DBs, decibels (volume of sound)

DINGLE, the branch of a tree, or similar object, held in front of a camera to give a foreground effect.

DISSOLVE, a gradual merging of one picture into another. Used to signify a lapse of time.

DISTAGON, a type of lens requiring a minimum of light.

DOLLY, a wheeled truck on which a camera is mounted.

DOLPHIN ARM, a mobile arm used for a film or small video camera, to take it up, down or sideways.

DOUBLE BANKING, to put one Studio Set in front of another. Time and space are saved when the front Set is removed to reveal a second ready constructed Set.

DOUBLE BROAD, a soft source of light with two incandescent lamps.

DOUBLE CLAD, scenery that can be shot from both sides.

DRESSING, the furniture, ornaments, pictures etc. placed in a Set to establish its period and character.

DRESS RUN, final Rehearsal before shooting.

DROP OUT, a momentary loss of contact between a Video Recording Head and Tape causing a white flash on a recorded picture. Sometimes necessitates a Studio Retake.

DRY, forgetting a line of dialogue.

DRY RUN, run through of a show without all the proper effects, practical fires, etc.

DUB, 1. to transfer various tracks of Recorded sound; dialogue, effects, and music; in order to make a single composite sound track. 2. To substitute a spoken translation of a foreign film.

ECLAIR, a 16mm film camera, much favoured for use in tight shooting areas, e.g. the back of a car.

EDITING, the process of selecting and piecing together the various shots in a programme. Applicable to both film and video.

E.E.T.P.U, Electrical Electronic Telecommunication and Plumbing Union.

EIGHTY FIVE, a conversion filter used when shooting daylight scenes that are being shot on film stock which has been balanced for artificial light.

E.F.P, Electronic Field Production. A two camera lightweight video unit used for drama production. A development of

E.N.G. (q.v.)

E.N.G, Electronic News Gathering. A lightweight mobile video unit, particularly useful for transmitting *live* news items.

ELEMAC, a much favoured film camera Dolly.

ESTABLISHING SHOT, a shot usually taken near the beginning of a scene to show the geography and other important elements.

EXT, exterior.

EXTRAS, Crowd Artists who do not speak dialogue and may not take individual direction, but who may sing well known songs or choruses and take part in unskilled or unchoreographed dances. An Extra who is asked to take individual direction, but not to speak, becomes a WALK ON I and will get additional payment, as will a WALK ON II who may take direction and speak a few unimportant words. Promotion to either WALK ON I or WALK ON II can take place during the production.

EYELINE, the direction of an Actor's look.

FACILITY FEE, when a private householder agrees to let a Television Company use his house or garden he will be paid a fee. This will vary from a small amount paid on the spot by the Production Manager for the use of parking space or a lavatory, to a larger amount, necessitating a contract when the property will be used for filming. Large Facility Fees will be paid for the use of Stately Homes, Aircraft, Ships, Railways and Rolling Stock.

FAVOUR, to see more of one person's face than that of another in the same shot. To give prominence to any part of a picture.

FIFTY FIFTY TWO SHOT, a picture that favours two Actors equally.

FILM INSERT, filmed material to be inserted into an electronically recorded programme.

FIRE LINE, a line on the Studio floor marking a space, between the Studio Sets and the Studio Wall, that must be kept clear for safety.

FISH EYE LENS, a very wide angle lens, which gives an effect similar to a convex mirror.

FISHING ROD/FISHPOLE, a small hand held microphone boom used when a platform boom is not practicable.

FISH TANK, the Director's Studio Gallery, which has a large window for looking down onto the Studio Floor.

FLAG, a rectangular piece of wood or card used to deflect light from the camera lens.

FLARE, light reflecting from a bright surface into the camera lens.

FLASHBACK, a scene depicting past events.

FLAT, a piece of Scenery.

FLIPPER, a hinged flat which can be swung in to provide additional backing, or swung out to clear a space for cameras, sound booms or lights.

FLOATER, a piece of scenery placed in for specific shots only.

FM, Floor Manager.

FLOOR PLAN, an aerial view to show the positioning of Scenery and Technical equipment in the Studio.

FLOPOVER, optical Effect in which the picture is shown reversed.

FLUFF, a hesitation or floundering in dialogue.

FLY, scenery hanging from fixed lines or a fixed rail can be "flown" in or out.

FOGGING, this takes place when light spills on to the film stock, and is caused either by a manufacturing fault, bad loading of the film magazine or a fault in the camera housing.

FOLD BACK, voice, music or sound effects fed through Studio equipment for Actors to hear.

F.O.M, Film Operations Manager.

F/G, foreground.

FWD, forward.

FRAME, 1. the picture limits within which the "Action" is included e.g. "Have you got his hand with the Gun in frame?" 2. A single photographic shot in a roll of film.

FREEZE FRAME, where a single frame is held to give the effect of freezing the action.

FRENCH BRACE, a foldable strut for holding a piece of scenery.

FRENCH FLAG, an attachment to a Lamp which gives greater control of light in a given area. A new A.F.M. heard a call from the Lighting Cameraman for a "French Flag", and returned from the Props Van apologising that they only had a Union Jack.

FRONT AXIAL PROJECTION, a form of projector mounted on a camera with mirror and reflecting screens to show slides or film integrated with Actors in the main picture.

F/Xs effects. 1. Visual or Special Effects, (smoke, windscreens shattering, etc.) 2. Recorded sound effects on Tape or Disc.

GAFFER, the Chief electrician.

GAFFER TAPE, wide strong adhesive tape used for securing cables, stands, etc., on the set.

GALLERY, Studio Control Room.

GALLOWS ARM, triangular frame hinged to a flat for hanging a curtain.

GANTRY, walkway in the upper part of the Studio, for access to scenery lines and lighting rigs.

GATE, the part of the camera through which each frame of film passes for exposure.

GHOSTING, apparent repetition of the image on the screen.

GLASS SHOT, a sheet of glass is placed in front of a static camera and additional scenery is painted onto it. e.g. An ornate ceiling for an interior Studio Set. (Also see Matte Shot).

GOBO, a large Flag (q.v.) used on a stand or clamp to protect the lens from direct strong light that would cause flare.

GRADING, matching the colour of sequential film shots.

GRID, the framework high in the studio ceiling, for holding scenery and lighting hoists.

GRIPS, the member of the film unit responsible for transporting and setting up the camera equipment e.g. Tracks and Dollies.

GUARD RAIL, the Safety Rail on a scenery Rostrum.

GUN-MIC, a directional microphone, which is handled like a gun.

GUIDE TRACK, a sound track recorded when filming, to serve as a guide during post synchronisation and not for use in the finished programme. Always verbally identified with the clapperboard. e.g. "53 take 4 Guide Track".

HAIR IN THE GATE, sometimes while the camera is operating, a tiny sliver of film stock is dislodged into the aperture, or "Gate", of the camera. This will appear on the print as a distracting small hair waving about on the edge of the screen when the film is shown. After each shot the Camera Assistant checks that the "Gate" is clear. When he sees a tiny shred of film in the aperture he will call out: "Hair in the Gate".

HARD LIGHT, light that produces dense well defined shadows.

HEADER, a scenery lintel or beam across an opening.

HEAD LAMP, a light mounted on a camera.

HEAD ROOM, the space between the top of an Actor's Head and the upper edge of the picture.

HERON, a two man Studio camera.

HIGH HAT, a low mounting for a film camera, in the form of a vertical cylinder with a flange.

HIGH KEY, high luminance (brightness), of picture.

HIGH LIGHT, a bright reflection.

H.M.I, high pressure Mercury Iodide light – popular for exterior filming.

HOT HEAD, a remote controlled camera mounting.

HOT SPOT, a bright patch in the picture.

I.B.A, Independent Broadcasting Authority.

IDIOT CARD, Prompt card placed out of vision for an Actor having difficulty with his lines.

INKY-DINK, a baby spotlight.

INLAY, an electronic method of combining two pictures.

INT, interior.

JELLY, lighting gelatine placed in front of a lamp.

JIB, the arm of a camera crane – not necessarily very large – that enables the camera to be moved fluidly up, down or sideways.

JUMP CUT, 1. a picture edit that by design or accident (see crossing the line) produces a shock effect. 2. The deletion of a section within a shot.

KEY LIGHT, the primary light source that gives shape and form to any person or object.

KICK, light can reflect or "kick" off a surface.

KILL, stop. Get rid of. "Kill that car noise", or "Kill that light".

KIRBY WIRE, a system of wires and harness used for simulated flying – as in "Peter Pan" or "Doctor Who".

L.E, Light Entertainment.

LIMPET, a film camera mounting, with large suction pads, used in particular for car shots to be taken from the bonnet or side doors.

LINE UP, 1. Preparing Electronic cameras to record. 2. Getting Actors or objects into position for a shot.

LIP SYNC, where lip movement and dialogue are synchronous (together).

LIVE, 1. Programmes transmitted directly as they happen to the viewers e.g. sports coverage is often live. 2. When a Studio camera is transmitting, but not necessarily broadcasting its picture. e.g. "Camera Two is Live in the Office Set." 3. An "open", or switched on microphone.

L/A, Low Angle.

L.P.U, Location Production Unit. A drama recording unit using one or two electronic cameras.

L.S, Long Shot.

LOW KEY, low luminance, (brightness) of picture.

LOW LOADER, a low trailer which can be towed with a car on board. This enables camera and lights to be positioned in a variety of positions, whilst the illusion of a travelling car is maintained.

80

MAGAZINE, the container for film in a camera.

MAN HOURS, the number of hours allocated for the construction and painting of scenery; based on the estimated amount of work a man can do in an hour. Man hours are costed at a standard rate to the programme budget.

MARKS, aids in the form of sticky tape or chalk marks on the ground. Used to help an Actor get into his correct position, or to "find his marks".

MARKING A SHOT, verbally identifying a film shot and then using the Clapperboard. When the sound recorder is running and the Film Camerman is ready he will call out to the Assistant to: "Mark it".

MASKING, to conceal, either deliberately with scenery, or by accident when one Actor masks another: "Can you move a touch left, you are masking Snodgrass behind you."

MASTER SHOT, the shot that covers a whole scene in terms of duration and relevant action.

MATTE, a form of "Glass Shot" (q.v.) used in filming to put in, or remove, a part of the picture. The process may involve several stages when refinements such as moving clouds are required.

MATTE BOX, a Bellows or Box mounted in front of the camera lens to hold camera mattes (masks) or gelatine filters, as well as providing an efficient lens shade.

MS, a medium or Mid shot – cutting above the waist.

MIC, Microphone.

MICKEY MOUSE, to synchronise background music with the action.

MICROPHONY, distortion of picture produced by sound waves.

MILEAGE, applied to production value or story content. e.g. "We should get a lot of mileage out of this scene".

MIRROR SHOT, lining up a shot using a mirror to reflect people or objects.

MIX, another word for Dissolve. Transition between one picture and another to denote passing time.

MOLE, a three man camera crane mounting.

MONITOR, a T.V. set either in the Gallery Control Room or in the Studio, showing the cameras output.

MONTAGE, a series of short sequences, or shots to convey varied action over a period of time.

MOTOROLA, a favoured type of Walkie Talkie (q.v.)

MOVIOLA, a Film Editor's machine for reproducing a small picture of the film, with its sound at normal volume.

M.U, Musicians Union.

MUTE, silent. Film without sound.

NAGRA, the sound recorder in most common use for filming.

N.A.T.T.K.E, National Association of Television Theatrical and Kine Employees. The Scene Crew's Union. Recently amalgamated into B.E.T.A (q.v.)

NEG, Film Negative.

NETWORK, all Stations. i.e. The B.B.C. throughout the country; not just Regional as say Cardiff or Glasgow. The I.T.V. companies throughout the country; not just local, as H.T.V. for Wales or S.T.V. for Scotland.

NODDY, slang for an Extra – because of his fee he cannot speak so nods. Also refers to the cutaway shot of an Interviewer nodding.

N.G, No Good. In particular applied to film takes.

OB, Outside Broadcast – refers to electronic cameras only.

O/N, Overnight.

O.O.V or O.V, out of vision.

OPTICAL, a technical process used in the film laboratories to achieve a variety of results i.e. superimposing lettering over film shots or flying Superman over the rooftops by laying one, two or more pieces of film on top of each other. Advertisements on television often use opticals very effectively.

O/R, Outside Rehearsal.

O.T.T, Over The Top. In particular can refer to an Actor's performance.

OUT TAKES, Takes that will not be used in the final version of the programme.

OVERCRANK, to run a film camera faster than normal, in order to give a slow motion effect when the film is shown at proper speed.

OVERLAY, putting a picture from one electronic camera into an area of a scene being shown by a second camera.

PADDING, additional material – dialogue or action – used to bring an underrunning programme up to the required length.

PAN, abbreviation from Panoramic. To rotate the camera through an Arc. Pan RT. Pan LT. Pan Up. Pan Down.

PANACAM, a Panavision video camera adapted to shoot with film lenses in order to give a film look on tape.

PEA LIGHTS, very small lights, e.g. for a Christmas tree or to help represent a distant night city skyline, when placed in a Studio Backcloth.

82

PED, the standard mobile pedestal mounting, on which an
electronic studio camera is fixed. Operated by a man, or
woman, the camera can be raised or lowered with a finger and
moved across the Studio floor with comparatively little effort.

P.B.U, Photo Blow Up.

P.C.R, Professional Casting Report

PICK UP, an additional shot to cover a scene that the Director feels
has been inadequately covered.

PILOT, a sample programme of a possible series.

PLOTTING, working out the Actors moves in Outside Rehearsal,
or in the Studio with the cameras.

P.O.V, point of view, i.e. what a character sees.

POLECAT, an expanding metal pole, which fits between floor and
ceiling, or between walls, for rigging lights on location
interiors.

PRAC, practical, e.g. "Is that bedside light prac?"

PREP, prepare, e.g. "The Designer has gone to prep the next
location."

PRIME LENS, a high quality lens requiring a minimum of light.

PULL FOCUS, the action of altering focus from foreground to
background and vice versa. Unless motivated by movement,
it can be distracting, as the audience becomes aware of the
camera.

PUP, a small hard light source.

Q, cue. A starting signal that can be given by a gesture, a light or
verbally.

RADIO MIC, a small microphone that can be concealed on a
Actor. A lead is attached to a small transmitter which is also
hidden in the Actor's clothing.

RATINGS, the estimated number of viewers.

RAW STOCK, unexposed film.

RECCE, Reconnaissance or Reconnoitre. 1. Looking for
locations. 2. Taking the film crew to determine lights needed,
etc.

REDHEAD, hard source lightweight lamp. often used as a hand
held light, e.g. when filming inside a travelling car.

REFLECTORS, lightweight boards, used to reflect sunlight
during filming. Sheets of polystyrene are also often used to
"bounce" light.

REGULARS, the Actors in a Series or Serial who are in all, or
most of the Episodes.

R/V, rendezvous e.g. "The R/V for the unit is "The Cat and Fiddle."

REPEATS, the second showing of a programme. This will mean Repeat Fees for the Actors.

RESIDUALS, fees from the sale of a programme abroad. These can be substantial if sold to the U.S.A., or so minimal as to be insignificant if sold to Third World countries.

REVERSE CUT, (see crossing the line).

RIFLE MIC, (see Gun Mic).

RISER, a low platform to raise an Actor, camera or furniture a few inches off the ground.

RIGGERS, the video outside broadcast crew who place cameras, put down tracking rails and lay out cables etc.

ROLLING BASE, a lightweight, rigid, three wheeled tripod, used by film and small video cameras on a smooth surface, when a free fluid movement is required.

ROUGH CUT, the first assembly of portions of film in correct sequence order.

RUNNING ORDER, the order in which scenes will be recorded.

RUNNING TIME, length of programme.

RUSHES, the first prints of film, processed overnight and viewed the next morning. Sometimes known as "Dailies".

SCANNER, name given to a Mobile Video Control Room.

SENNHEISER, a much favoured hand held gun microphone.

SET, 1. To place in position. 2. Arrangement of scenery to represent a room or place.

SET UP, the film camera's position e.g. "The next set up is over here".

SHOOT, 1. The action of taking pictures. 2. The overall period of filming e.g. "How did the shoot go?"

SHOOTING RATIO, the amount of film stock used relative to the finished edited product. The average shooting ratio for filmed drama is 10 to 1. i.e. Ten minutes of film stock will be used to create an edited sequence lasting one minute. The shooting ratio for documentaries is considerably higher – sometimes 30 to 1.

SHOT, the picture taken by a camera e.g. "Location Shot"; a film shot taken on a location away from the Studio.

SHOT NUMBER, the sequential number given to each shot for identification purposes.

SHOW PRINT, the final film print for Transmission, in which all the grading is acceptable.

SILL IRONS, the strips of metal fixed across the foot of scenery doors to strengthen them; particularly in transit from scenery contractors to the Studio.

SIMON HOIST, a mobile aerial camera platform. Some are capable of a height of 150 feet. (See Cherry Picker).

SINGLE CLAD, scenery to be seen from one side only, as opposed to Double Clad.

SKY, to raise; as in "Sky the Boom" between shots in the Video Studio.

SLATE, 1. The Clapperboard. 2. To slate: to use the clapperboard e.g. Slate 53 Take 4.

SLOT, the placing of a programme in the Schedules. e.g. "We've got the nine o'clock slot on Saturdays."

SLUNG MIC, a fixed suspended microphone.

SNAKE, a piece of equipment that can be attached to the elemac dolly (q.v.), to obtain low shots.

SNOOT, a funnel shaped fitting for a light, used to vary the size and shape of a beam.

SOFT LIGHT, light that produces faint ill-defined shadows if any.

S.O.F, Sound on Film.

SPARKLE, white speckling on film, normally caused by dirt on the negative.

SPARKS, Electricians.

SPECIAL HIGH/LOW, applicable at the B.B.C. to fees which take into account the importance of a role relative to the Actor's normal fee.

SPEED, the Film Sound Recordist's call when his recorder is running at the correct speed.

SPIDER BOX, a Junction Box for a number of lights.

SPILL, unwanted light.

SPOT EFFECTS, sound effects put in live during a performance.

SPREADER, a flat wooden or plastic base consisting of three folding arms, used for supporting a camera tripod on slippery non-grip surfaces, like marble floors.

SPYDER, the wheel base of the Elemac Dolly.

STABLE, the list of Actors with an Agent. e.g. "Whose Stable are you in?"

STAGGER THROUGH, the first effort to run a scene with Studio Cameras, usually involving frequent stops to correct errors.

STAND IN, a person who is doubling for a performer, particularly when shots are being lit, or lined up during rehearsal.

STAND MIC, a microphone on a stand.

STEADICAM, a special camera mounting attached to the cameraman to give fluid movement when doing hand held shots – particularly when going up or down stairs.

STEENBECK, a film editing and viewing machine.

STILL, a photograph taken by a Stills Camera.

STOCK SET, a set which is kept for constant use.

STOCK SHOT, a library shot.

STOOGING, when a character is in shot, but has no dialogue or business necessary to the plot.

STRIKE, to remove scenery or an object from a Set.

STROBING, a streaking, juddering effect caused by Television frequencies beating in time, Venetian blinds, wheel patterns, zig zags, and herringbone patterns often cause strobing.

SUGAR GLASS, a harmless, realistic substitute used for windows, glasses, picture glass etc., when it is required to be broken by or near an Actor or Camera.

SUN GUN, a hand held battery lamp.

SWINGER, a piece of scenery hinged to another.

SYNC, to coincide the picture with the sound track, in particular to synchronise lip movements with dialogue e.g. "I don't think that the sound is in sync with the picture".

SYPHER, post dubbing sound for a videotaped programme. (See Dubbing).

TAKE, to shoot a shot or a sequence of shots.

TARIFF, apparatus to rectify colour grading errors in film or video.

TECH-RUN, a Run through for Technicians at Outside Rehearsal.

TELECINE, film projection in Televison.

TENDER, a vehicle for transporting heavy equipment.

TEN LIGHT, soft light source of ten incandescent lamps.

THROWN, when an Actor's concentration is broken he is "Thrown".

TILT, to tip the camera through a vertical Arc ("Tilt up", "Tilt down").

TIME CODE, an electronic signal, which is controlled by the time of the Studio clock, and is printed onto a track on all Drama Video tapes whilst recording, in order to assist with editing. The Time Code can be made visible on the lower part of the picture and takes up a very small percentage of the screen. Every frame of the 25 video frames per second is marked. Thus the eighth frame taken at 3.00pm. 32 minutes and ten seconds will be marked: 15.32.10.08. The Director can take home a video cassette of all programme material and note Time code editing points to save time when assembling the Master Tape with the V.T. Editor in the Editing suite.

TITAN, a large eight man camera crane.

TOP HAT, (See High Hat).

TOP SHOT, a shot taken from immediately, or nearly overhead.

TRACK, forward or backward movement of a camera. e.g. "Track in or Track out".

TRACK LAYING, to synchronise different sound sources on different sound tracks, for mixing onto a master track.

T AND D, Travel and Duty Expenses.

TRAP, (See Camera Trap).

TRIMS, unused remnants of film shots after editing.

TRI-TRACK, a form of rolling base (q.v.)

TURN OVER, the Director's instruction for the film camera to start turning.

TWO FOUR SIXES, tiered wooden blocks with heights of two, four and six inches – used for heightening furniture in the Studio.

TX, transmission.

UNDER CRANK, to run the film through the camera at a slower than normal rate, which will give the effect of faster moving action when shown at proper speed.

UNIT, all the crew involved in a given production's filming, e.g. "The Unit Call for tomorrow is 0700".

VARITOL, a type of zoom lens.

V.C.R, Video Cassette Recorder.

V.H.S, Video Home Service.

VIGNETTE, a cut out shape placed in front of the camera to mask out part of the scene, e.g. to give a keyhole or binocular effect.

VIZ. F/X, Visual Effects. Realistic dummies, fires, explosions, smoke, breaking furniture, trick props, cobweb machines, chemical effects, etc. Also known as Special Effects.

V.O, Voice over. i.e. Narration over picture.

V.T, Videotape. In particular refers to the V.T. Area where the recording machines operate. During the Studio Recording the Technical Operations Manager will instruct the V.T. Operator, via a talkback system, to "Run V.T."

WALKIE TALKIE, small, hand held, battery operated, two-way radio equipment used by production personnel for audio communication during filming.

WALK ON, (See EXTRAS).

WALK THROUGH, first rehearsal on the Set, when the Director describes the scene in detail to the Actors and Crew.

WHIP PAN, to pan the camera very fast.

WILD TRACK, a sound track recorded separately from any picture or pictures with which it may subsequently be combined.

WING, when an Actor makes up dialogue to try and cover a fluff or a dry.

WORKING COPY, see Cutting Copy.

WOW, a slow variation in pitch of recorded sound.

WRAP, to complete filming for that specific day or night. The Production Manager calls: "It's a wrap."

W/A, Wide Angle.

W.S, Wide Shot.

X, to cross. e.g. George X R – George crosses camera right.

XLS, Extreme Long Shot. e.g. a distant landscape in which figures will appear relatively small.

ZIP UP, a collapsible tower of varying height that can be used as a platform for camera or lights.

ZOOM, a lens with a continuously variable angle over a defined range. e.g. $5^0 - 50^0$.

Index

The Index is relevant to the main text. The Glossary, in addition to covering some of the indexed items in more detail, also lists many other terms, abbreviations and phrases.

90

Dr Who, 22
Drinks, 59
Driving, 16, 40
Dubbing, 71
Dundee, 36

Editing video, 7, 69
Editor (Film), 11, 33, 42, 58, 69
Editor (Script), 10, 11, 45-48, 53, 61
E.E.T.P. Union, 36
Effects (sound), 59, 71
Effects (visual), 28, 39
Electricians, 11, 36, 57, 58
Electronics, 1
Electronic cameras, 44, 64
Electronic (video) studio, 1, 20, 26, 28, 44, 62-69
Elizabethan, 37
Emphasis, 32, 37, 51, 52, 59
Engineers, 1
Equipment (camera), 33, 34, 56, 58, 64
Equipment (lighting), 36, 63, 64
Episodes of series, 10, 20, 21, 67
Equity, 7, 8
Executive Producer, 10, 12
Expenses, 18, 24, 30
Explosions, 38
Exteriors, 32, 42, 44, 71
Extras (walk-ons, crowd artists), 8, 67

Facility fee, 17
Falls (stunt), 39
Fares (travelling), 24
Feature films, 4, 21
Fees, 5, 19-21, 24
Fights, 39
Filing cabinets, 59
Film Crew, 11, 28, 30, 31, 32
Film Editor, 11, 33, 42, 58, 69
Film inserts, 69
Filming, 17, 18, 19, 23, 24, 26, 27-46
Film locations, 11, 17, 20, 24, 26, 28, 29, 30, 32, 37, 42, 45, 47
Film Operations Manager, 42
Film operatives, 38
Film Unit, 24, 29, 30, 31, 39, 42
Firearms, 37, 39
Fire-brigade, 41
Fires, 38, 40
Fire tongs, 37
First Aid kit, 18
First Assistant Director (Production Manager), 17

Floor Assistant, 66
Floor Manager, 64, 66, 68, 69
Floor plan (studio), 56, 57
Fluff (artists'), 33
Flowers, 59
Focus (camera), 33
Food, 41, 59
Foreign filming, 24
Foreign Legion, 36
Foreign Office, 14
Framing, 33, 34
Furniture, 37, 38, 51, 62, 66

Gaffer (lighting chargehand), 36
Gallery (studio), 17, 18, 59, 64, 66, 68, 69
General interview, 3
Gestures, 52
Glasgow, 4
Grid (studio), 64
Grips (i/c film camera equipment), 33
Guests in a series, 10
Guns, 39
Gun Mics, 34

Hair, 23, 30
Hang-glide, 16
Hats, 62
Head of Channel, 12
Head of Department, 10, 12, 28
Health, 24
Henry V, 6
Hepburn, Audrey, 8
High Hat, 34
Hoists (lighting), 63
Hollywood, 8, 16
Horses, 39
Horse riding, 16
Hospitals, 29
Hotels, 24, 28, 30
Human factor, 1

Ident Board (studio), 68
Images, 51
Independent Television Companies, 4, 8, 9, 13, 19, 21, 27, 36, 47, 62, 67, 68
Injections, 24
Inserts (Film), 69
Inserts (Studio), 69
Instinct, 52
Intercutting shots, 53, 57, 59, 60
Interiors (film), 37, 42